The Gingerbread House

The Gingerbread House

A journey of faith through bereavement

Esther Shreeve

British Library Cataloguing in Publication data

A catalogue record for this book is available
from the British Library

ISBN 1 85852 280 3

First published by Inspire
4 John Wesley Road
Werrington
Peterborough PE4 6ZP

Printed and bound in Great Britain by
Cromwell Press, Trowbridge

Dedication

For Chris, Sarah and Nathan, with my love

Acknowledgements

This book could not have been written without the support of many people. At the time of Ben's death I do not know how we would have managed without the practical help of our friends Gwen and Noel Clark, Janet and Mark Facer, Clare and Boris Anderson, Pauline and Dave Kendall, Ken and June Hebborn, and Kingsley and Margaret Barrett. Hilary Minter was our bereavement counsellor and we owe her a great debt. As the book began to take shape, various people played their part: the poetry of Jessica Aidley transformed what I was trying to do; Gail Kerry, Deborah McVey, Lesley-Ann Knox and my sister, Ruth Grayson, were able to lend their professional expertise as well as provide me with a critical audience. Finally, my family bore with me as I revisited and reflected on painful memories, and encouraged me along every step of the way.

Contents

Introduction

I used to keep a diary, writing in it as often as I could. It wasn't meant to be a 'reflective journal' of the kind students who are training for ministry in the Church are encouraged to keep; rather, it was an account of day-to-day life, which I thought might be interesting to look back on in later years. The reflection came later! I began the process when I was engaged and working in Papua New Guinea; my fiancé was in Sierra Leone, and good communications were vital to enable our relationship to develop. Letters took a long time (sometimes as much as three months), so we were both keen to describe the pattern of our lives as fully as possible to one another – hence the diary. Three years after we returned to the United Kingdom, I was still diarizing; it is what I wrote around the time of the birth and death of our second child, Ben Paul, which forms much of the raw material for this book (and appears in italics in the text). Fourteen years later, both my brother and one of my husband's brothers died within a few months of each other; what we felt and experienced then is another part of my engagement with bereavement; different, yet also familiar.

'Raw' is, in many ways, the operative word. This is an account of, and reflection on, a journey through grief, and my diary evokes the pain and desolation of that time. Only a few months after the death of our baby son, I knew that one day I would want to write more about it, but I had to wait until the time was right. Simply to describe what had happened was not enough; there had to be a context and a purpose to what I wrote. What that would be was not immediately apparent. Over the years, as my life has moved on, I have developed a perspective on my experience of grief which relates closely to the facts that I am a Christian, and married to a minister. We have lived in very rural situations, where the minister is quite a public person, and this has brought its own particular pressures. Should not my faith have helped me, and be seen to help me, deal with loss rather more positively and painlessly than if I had had no faith? Yet, far from being able to take refuge in the great truths of Christianity, I found myself questioning the very foundation of my beliefs. My faith and spirituality were deeply challenged, in a way that had never happened before. The sense of being in the public eye as we experienced a major personal crisis brought certain additional pressures into play of which I think we were only dimly aware at the time. There are a lot of myths around about how Christians should deal with loss; we have learned that there is no right way to grieve, nor is there necessarily an immediately recognizable resolution to the toil that is part of the process.

When I told friends what I was doing, many of them suggested that I should talk to other people who had also experienced the loss of a child. I resisted this, because I wanted this to be a personal reflection, and not a general, and therefore more objective, description of a particular kind of bereavement. But I did follow up one lead; I had met Jessica Aidley some years ago, and was shocked to hear of the sudden and untimely death of her husband in the summer of 2000. What I did not know was that she had found an outlet for her grief in writing poetry, and virtually chronicled her journey through bereavement in verse. None of this has yet been published, but Jessica has kindly given me permission to use some of her poetry in this book. She has a gift I wish I had; I have used her work where it seemed particularly appropriate, because she can articulate emotion so vividly, in a way that my prose lacks. I look forward to the day when her poetry is published in its own right.

I offer this book in the hope that it may be of help to those who are living with bereavement, or anyone caring for the bereaved. It also puts down some markers about expectations surrounding people in public ministry in the Church. There have been times when I have been alongside others who are dealing with some grim situations; it has not been appropriate to talk about myself, but I have sometimes wished I could put a book into their hands that might strike a chord with them. One of the most important things that I discovered when I was on my own journey is that it is not helpful to try to compare grief with grief, and it can be positively *un*helpful to try to exercise pastoral care based on particular anecdotal experiences of someone else who 'got through it' this or that way, because of the guilt that may follow when it doesn't work like that for the person concerned. This is not intended to offer a blueprint for dealing with grief or crisis; it certainly is not an academic textbook about either the grief process, or the theology of suffering! It is a personal and, I hope, honest, reflection on how it was, and is still, for me.

1

Marriage, Ministry and Motherhood

It began with a family treat trip out, down the road from our home in Hawes to a café that had just opened. It was my husband's birthday; his mother was visiting, and it was an excuse for a celebration. I ordered a cup of tea and a scone, and was sitting, reflecting on how very weary I felt, and how surprisingly unappetizing the scone looked, when I glanced down and observed that I was wearing a pair of unmatching shoes. They were not spectacularly different, simply representing new and old vintages of moccasins. But it was a shock. I was feeling very tired and rather spaced out. The penny dropped – could it be possible that I was pregnant? Surely not. This wasn't planned; I was still breastfeeding Sarah, who was only ten months old, and my heart most certainly did not leap for joy at the prospect of another baby so soon.

Over the next few months, we tried to get excited about 'Junior', as we called my slowly growing bump. We might not have intended to extend the family immediately, but since it had happened, we would work hard to ensure that we would welcome the baby, as we had Sarah. After all, I persuaded myself, there must be advantages in having one's children so close together – a concentration of sleepless nights, nappies, slow toddling expeditions to the playground, shops and surrounding countryside. I didn't feel that I was a natural earth mother, and although I knew I wanted to have a family, it was the hardest and most challenging thing I had ever done. Without the support of my husband Chris, who is superb with small children, I would have sunk without trace. He, too, was shocked to discover that we were having another baby, and somewhat anxious as to how on earth we would manage.

We were under a lot of pressure. This was hardly surprising, in view of events over the previous two years; we had married only eight months after my father had died. In the 18 months before our wedding we had seen very little of each other, as Chris was working for the Methodist Church in Sierra Leone, and I had been in Papua New Guinea, prior to my father's stroke in August 1985. Our courtship at Kingsmead College in Selly Oak had been a whirlwind affair back in the autumn of 1984. We both felt we were committed to our jobs overseas, so we decided to get engaged and then go our separate ways for a couple of years. After the wedding, the hard work began: we had to get to know each other and to learn to live together. Chris was stationed as Methodist minister in Hawes, a market town at the top end of Wensleydale, and we set up home in a very spacious and rather chilly house, which boasted eight buckets in the attic, to catch the drips when it rained – and there is a lot of rain in that part of the world! It was most exciting when, some time in 1987, our respective boxes and trunks arrived from overseas; we unpacked them together, and discovered what we had each brought to the marriage. Our cats were most impressed by the snakeskin which emerged from one of Chris's trunks; Customs and Excise had had to be reassured that the snake had already been killed (it was dangerous!) and had not paid the ultimate price just to be brought home as a trophy.

Our respective friends were keen to meet the other half of the partnership, and we had a constant stream of visitors, which kept me occupied, and helped me deal with the strange situation of not having a job. I wrestled with a real identity crisis, as I discovered what it might mean to be the minister's wife. It was not easy to make friends; most of the people in our congregations were at least a generation older than we were, and it felt as if we had moved into a very close-knit community. At least Chris wasn't new to ministry, but rural Methodism was an unknown phenomenon to me, and would take some getting used to. He was welcomed and accepted because he was the minister. As his wife I too had a particular position, but I wasn't sure I wanted it! I had expectations of the way I should fulfil the role, partly based on my own upbringing (my father was a minister), and I also had ideas about the way in which I thought I would be perceived by others; I was about to enter a minefield. Perhaps if I had been at theological college with Chris at the time when he was training, I might have been better prepared; as it was, I had married a fully fledged and experienced minister, although he had only had experience of the role as a single man, not a married one.

When we were first married, I was simply not aware of the power that expectations can wield in our lives. Every day was full and varied, and we lived very much from day to day without, at first, even seeing the need to stop and reflect; later, when it became apparent that we would have to, it was difficult to find the time and space for what was a very fluid agenda item. Expectations can cause a lot of headaches, not least because they are often unspoken or even subconscious, and therefore hard to recognize or acknowledge. This was true both of my own expectations of myself and those I had of others, and of the expectations which other people may have had of me. Since I have resumed my professional career, I have found it quite liberating and empowering to negotiate my own job description as part of the professional appraisal process I participate in annually, because it makes me and my colleagues ferret away at what expectations are attached to what we do. We all recognize that this is important, and helpful, and make sure that there is space for it in our diaries. But it is rare, I think, to find clergy who are working according to set job descriptions; many ministers would hotly deny that they are, in fact, doing a job at all. It is therefore not to be wondered at that most clergy partners of my generation would, I suspect, strongly resent and resist any attempt to give them a job description. They have my sympathy! One still comes across the notion of the wife being the 'unpaid curate'; this is thankfully less common than it was because of the number of clergy partners, many of whom are men, who are working in paid employment. But this was not the case 19 years ago, or certainly not in rural areas, although things have changed a great deal even in this short space of time.

At this stage, I did not have a paid job, and I fully expected to be active in the life of our eight churches. The problem was in finding a role that fitted; for a start, I was so much younger than the vast majority of our congregations. I felt uneasy about becoming the president of the various women's groups which met regularly, because I had no experience of them and they felt quite alien. So I declined, and it was a relief that this seemed to be quite acceptable; quite probably I had only been asked because the minister's wife had traditionally always done it, and people had reservations about my fitness for the job anyway! Coffee mornings appeared regularly on the social calendars of our churches, and I was happy to bake contributions; I had always thought I was reasonably proficient, but when I encountered the productions of experts, the farmers' wives who had been honing the art of baking to perfection since they were children, I retreated hastily. We consumed what I made at home, and enjoyed it, even if I did not dare produce anything in public. In my more paranoid moments, I blamed the temperamental second-hand oven that we had inherited with the house; Methodist church houses come with carpets, curtains and cookers, and you are lucky if you get new ones! Beyond that, as long as I was happy to answer the phone, pass on messages to Chris, help him with any administration he was able to delegate, appear with him regularly at various public occasions, and of course attend church and welcome all and sundry into our home, I was apparently doing what I was expected to do.

But I still had to deal with what I expected of *myself*, as a minister's wife, and that was a complicated mess of contradictions and impossibilities. Sometimes what I said, and what I actually felt or did, simply did not match up. In theory, I realized I could not possibly do, or be, all that I expected of myself; in practice I still tried. This, I may say, is still the case on occasion. I could formulate a plan of action, then find myself doing something completely contradictory; it was as if my instincts, influenced by deep-rooted subconscious expectations which I had not articulated even to myself, had taken over. This was particularly the case when I decided that I was *not* going to do something, because there were other, perfectly valid, claims on my time, or I simply did not have the energy – and then found myself doing it anyway. I am now much more aware of the problem than I used to be, but that doesn't mean that I have solved it. I do so want to keep people happy!

Finding the courage to say 'no' was a particular and immediate problem; we had, at the beginning, a constant stream of visitors. Everyone, it seemed, wanted to call on the new minister and his wife and spy out the land; we wanted to be as hospitable as we could, but there were times when it was all too much.

Getting days off together, for example, appeared to be practically impossible; it took us several months to realize that we had to sit down with the calendar and block a day off each week, months in advance, if we were to be sure of having it. It was so tempting to think we could just squeeze in a particular visit or event; the relief of waking up on a day when we knew there was nothing in the diary for either of us was immense. But then we would have to go out for the day to be sure of keeping it for ourselves, which meant that the list of jobs to do at home got steadily longer, and that then brought its own pressures. The root of the problem lies, I think, in the notion of pastoral care which a minister is expected to exercise; there is never an end to the list of people who expect, or need, attention!

Traditionally, the tendency has been to put the clergy family on a pedestal, and in the spotlight at the same time. In rural communities this is probably even more likely to happen. I well remember the response from our milkman when he learned that we were expecting Sarah: 'Well, you were trying hard enough, weren't you?' When we enquired what he meant, he said that he had observed that the curtains upstairs were always closed. The fact that he was commenting on the rooms at the front of the house while our bedroom was at the back, and that we kept our thermally lined curtains firmly shut to conserve heat, hadn't dawned on him. He lived in a cosy, modern bungalow!

Milkman notwithstanding, because of our ages when we married (I was 31 and Chris 38), we felt the pressure of the biological clock, and decided to try to start our family reasonably soon. This was one reason why I had not looked for work when we had settled in. On Christmas Day 1986 I discovered I was pregnant, and Sarah was born the following August.

We were delighted, but had not appreciated quite how much our lives were going to change – yet again. I wonder if anyone really does. But we had barely got our balance from the upheavals of the last two years and in terms of potential stress factors, we had really notched them up – bereavement, various moves, changes of job (and in my case giving up work), marriage, and starting a family.

Nor was my first pregnancy particularly easy. I experienced all-day sickness, which lasted for the entire pregnancy, had a very long labour, then had to deal with a postnatal infection alongside problems in establishing breastfeeding with a colicky baby. I will never forget the time I ventured to leave my newborn baby and take a bath when I was on the maternity ward, and hearing, above the noise of the running water, the already familiar sound of my daughter crying. The problem was not so much that she was crying (even *I* knew that babies did that), but the realization that she was *my* responsibility, and that no one else would rescue her.

I was something of a physical and emotional wreck, and with hindsight would hazard a guess that for some months I suffered a degree of postnatal depression. Either that, or simple culture shock! On one occasion Chris was spotted coming out of the local off-licence clutching a six-pack of Guinness, which the midwife had suggested that I try to boost my milk supply. He walked straight into an elderly couple – staunch teetotallers – who were stalwarts at one of our chapels. When they looked at him askance, he hastily explained that the stout had been prescribed, not for a moment letting on that actually I was thoroughly enjoying it, and that we did not in fact subscribe to the wing of the church which frowned upon alcohol. Thankfully the wife had been given the same instructions by her doctor with her own babies, and had taken it 'as medicine'. Expectations again!

Chris kept me, and Sarah, going, along with everything that went with pastoral charge of eight rural chapels. Those days were hard work, and exhausting. I dreaded the times when Chris would be away all day; I know that I could never have survived being at home on my own with a baby for five or six days a week, as many mothers have to, still less being a single parent. We were just beginning to emerge, and to enjoy being a family unit, when we discovered that another baby was on the way. Ben Paul was born just 17 months after Sarah. Although he had not been planned, the devastation of his death turned our world upside down.

2

The Howl Within

The howl within
Does not come from broken bones,
or bruised skin;
It comes from the being torn in two,
In the losing of you.

Try as I might, I simply could not muster up any feelings of anticipation or excitement about the new arrival, which was due on 12 January. One day, early in December, I went into the spare bedroom and retrieved the bag of first-size baby clothes that I had put away after Sarah had grown out of them. I washed them all, and put them up to dry on the pulley that hung in the kitchen; they looked very tiny and cute, and had some lovely memories attached to them. But all I could feel as I looked up was a real heaviness of heart, even dread. Was this because I could not imagine what it would be like to have two children?

I tried to share some of my misgivings with a friend. She reassured me that she had experienced something similar; she could not believe that she would be able to love her second child as much as she did her first. But when her second son was actually born, she felt she began to understand something of the boundless love of God; there was absolutely no problem in loving both children; God's love is infinite, and a parent's love reflects that. That helped to some extent, but my niggling doubts continued. We had some photographs developed that we had taken in Edinburgh when we went to the zoo;

although I was seven months pregnant, I looked very slim, with my coat zipped up as normal.

On 14 December I had to take Sarah to the doctor because she had an ear infection. I wrote afterwards:

> *He took the opportunity to examine me, and commented that either I am very neat, or the baby is rather small, but that the head is engaged, so that delivery could happen any time. I have not put on any weight, but he does not see that as cause for concern; I should go home and get things ready. I didn't feel I could tell him about my worries – I am not even sure what my worries were. I just feel a strong sense of foreboding.*

Did I sense instinctively that something was wrong, or was I just working out my feelings because this baby had not been planned? I simply did not know.

On our last day off before Christmas, we seized the opportunity to make a gingerbread house. This is part of my family's tradition, from the German side; it is based on the story of Hansel and Gretel, and their encounter with the wicked witch who lured them to her home which was made of gingerbread and covered in sweets. This inspired the custom of families making gingerbread houses as part of their preparations for Christmas. We did this every year when I was a child, and I loved it; now that Sarah was old enough to enjoy it, we inaugurated the tradition in our own new family. I got the recipe for the gingerbread from my mother, and proceeded to bake it; when it was cold and firm, I instructed Chris in what he had to do, namely take on the role of architect, structural engineer and then builder. I doubted my own ability in this direction, but kept him plied with suggestions and cocktail sticks as he constructed the little house. Meanwhile, I made a large bowlful of royal icing, which we plastered on the roof and walls; then Sarah helped us to attach the sweets. A wonderful, blissfully sticky time ensued. We were grateful for a heating system that guaranteed us hot water all the time, because we all needed a bath afterwards.

Christmas preparations were in full swing by then. We had recently acquired our first computer, and Chris was determined to get our address book on it; that way, he argued, sending out our Christmas cards would be so much easier. In the midst of the round of Christmas dinners and carol services, he fiddled with the machine, trying to get it to print out the labels so that the complete address actually appeared in the middle of the label. He got hot and bothered, and I was immensely frustrated, knowing how quickly I could have done it by hand. Eventually I retired to bed, and let him get on with it.

On the evening of 16 December I was delighted to get a phone call from a friend telling me that she was pregnant; they had had a long wait to get to this point because of various genetic problems. As I talked to her I realized that I was feeling rather uncomfortable; was this trapped wind, or was I feeling early contractions? Chris came in from a carol service, looking like death warmed up, and reported he had a migraine. We felt we could have done without anything happening that evening, but it was not to be. Choosing when to go into labour is a luxury most people do not have! By 10 o'clock I was fairly sure I had started, so we wrapped Sarah in her duvet and took her next door, where our neighbours, Gwen and Noel, already had a cot waiting. We set off for the hospital, and I was very grateful for the warmed seat which our car offered. As we got to the roundabout outside Northallerton, around midnight, I said to Chris I feared there would be something wrong with the baby. He just nodded and replied, 'This baby will change our lives.'

17 December. This is/was the day Benjamin Paul was born (4lbs 14oz) and died. It doesn't seem very real, but writing about him may help. I wasn't altogether surprised when labour started, after yesterday's twinges. It is odd the way we have both felt fearful about what is to come, and somehow we've always known that there would be something different about this pregnancy.

The labour was very quick, and easily managed. We had only been at the hospital for half an hour before Ben was born; I got rather irritated with the Sister, who would insist on hooking me up to a monitor, and wouldn't let me kneel when I wanted to, but she had obviously recognized that there were complications. Ten contractions, a few puffs of gas and air, a push, and there he was, weighing in at nearly five pounds. The room was suddenly full of people, who may have come in as I was in labour, or perhaps after I had given birth; it all happened so quickly I honestly do not know at what stage they arrived. I reached for Ben, to put him to my breast as I had done with Sarah (suddenly it felt as if her birth was only yesterday), but he was quite blue and they whipped him away to a cot in a corner of the room while they worked on him and put him on a ventilator. Apparently he did try to breathe on his own, and sucked the young doctor's finger, as she willed him to live. The paediatric consultant burst into the room, wearing an overcoat over his pyjamas, and took control. We were left to ourselves, shocked and wondering. Chris had seen more of him than I had, and had noticed a facial disfigurement – he had a double cleft palate. Eventually they took him away to Special Care while we sat and waited, bewildered. Then the consultant came back and told us what he thought was wrong. Ben probably had Trisomy 13, meaning he had three copies of chromosome 13 instead of the normal two copies, and basically everything was haywire – heart defect, liver and kidney problems, double cleft palate, and six digits on each of his hands and feet. He would probably be severely mentally retarded as well. A blood test would confirm it, but he was sure that this was the case. He told us he didn't think he could live long at all, and that his condition was incompatible with life. We didn't hesitate, but asked for the life support to be stopped, and little Ben was brought to us, wrapped in a shawl, and laid in my arms. He was so peaceful, we don't actually know when he died, but Chris baptized him with water from the jug on my bedside cabinet while we had him. Sister Wilkinson was a bit nonplussed by that; she arrived a few minutes later with a proper box containing all the baptismal bits, holy water, oil, a crucifix, and a Prayer Book! We did it more for our sakes than for his – we know that he is with God now and supremely well, and also that his baptism wasn't his passport to heaven. But we needed to do all we could for him in the very short time we had him, and this was something we could do to show our love for him.

It was a question of using the very limited time we had with him to the full.

After a while I was moved to a small private room, and Chris was given a camp bed beside me. A sleepless night followed, but it was good to be together, so we could talk and weep as we wished. We were given a Polaroid photo, which was very helpful; for a while it seemed as if this hadn't happened, and the photo gave us a sense of reality. One of the nursing auxiliaries was wonderful; she came and asked us if we would like to have Ben for another cuddle. My instinctive reaction was one of recoil, but I remembered what various friends had said to me about their own experiences when they had lost their babies, and I knew that I would regret not seeing him and holding him again. Now I wish we had had longer with him; I couldn't quite muster the courage to look at him properly, and see his hands and feet with his 12 fingers and toes. Talking with friends who work as hospital chaplains, it seems that today it is standard practice to encourage parents and even other members of the family to spend time with a baby who has died, whether that is a stillbirth or a neonatal death, such as Ben's (see Afterword). Some people have even taken their baby home with them for a while; I am not sure that I could have done that, yet it might have been good to have given our families the chance to see him, which they never had. Chris had rung them in the early hours, needing to share our immediate grief with them, but they were too far away to be able to come quickly even if they had wanted to. We were fortunate in that we both had families we could contact, and that we knew they would care; we were to discover what an isolating phenomenon grief can be, and would need all the support we could find to help us in the days to come.

3

Raw Grief

17 December was a long day. It took until early afternoon to complete the necessary paperwork at the hospital, and for the doctor to see me and declare me fit to go home. We had had no idea that so much bureaucracy would be involved, but it was perhaps no bad thing that we were given a few quiet hours together, to begin to take on board what had happened, before we had to face the world.

We began to think about the funeral; I struggled with what we should do, but we knew we had to do something. I was grateful that Ben had been born alive; I think we might have found things more difficult if he had been stillborn, although thankfully things have changed in the last 15 years. We needed to honour his life, and decide what to do with his body, but was it 'done' to have a funeral for a baby who had only lived for an hour? Chris's experience was that this was indeed in order; the question then was whether we should have a very quiet, private service for the family, or whether it should be open to our friends. In the end, we decided on a compromise; we would have a service at the chapel in Hawes which would be open to all, and then a private family cremation. We felt instinctively that many people would want to come to share our grief and show their support for us. The impact of Sarah's birth had taken us by surprise; she was the first baby born to a minister in Hawes for as long as anyone could remember; for weeks after her birth people would come up to us and put silver coins under her mattress in the pram, which meant we quickly had to open a building society account for her! To some extent, we were public property, and it would be easier to face people if we did not hide the funeral away from them.

We left the hospital feeling utterly empty, and in the lift we met the parents of someone in Hawes who had just had a baby. They had obviously heard our news (the bush telegraph is an amazing thing); none of us knew where to put ourselves, and a lift is a small place. We got home about 3 p.m. to find our first visitor on the doorstep. She didn't stop, simply pressing a tin of mince pies into our hands, which proved extremely useful over the next few days, as people called in.

We were longing to see Sarah, whom we had bundled next door so very unceremoniously the night before. When we went in she was holding court to Gwen and Noel, sitting in her high chair brandishing a spoon. She had clearly had a wonderful time, but was quite happy to come home. It was somewhat strange to realize that she could have very little comprehension of what had happened; as far as she was concerned life was going on as normal, although we did try to explain to her, in as matter of fact a way as we could, where we had been and why there would be no baby coming to keep her company. It was a question of gently unpicking what we had been preparing her for over the last few weeks, but it seemed that she really had not taken much of that on board, so not much needed to be said now. The occasional reminder of why Mummy and Daddy were sad was sufficient. It is interesting that today she observes that she remembers being very perplexed because of the apparent disappearance of my stomach; she wondered how I was going to eat.

Visitors and phone calls came in thick and fast. A couple of friends from Newton Aycliffe just dropped by, having no idea what had happened; another friend arrived, white as a sheet, offering nothing but her presence and love – which meant everything. My sister, Ruth, abandoned her own young family and came hotfoot from Sheffield; she took over the reins of the household, which helped enormously. It's as well that I have never minded other people making themselves at home in 'my' kitchen – it comes with not being house-proud, I guess. Our GP called in, and stayed a surprisingly long time, which we really appreciated. We had the sense that this was someone who knew what he was talking about and who had our best interests at heart; he was particularly concerned for Chris, which was reassuring to me as I had already sensed that most people would be concentrating on me. Yes, I was the one who had gone through the physical experience of giving birth, and who would have to deal with the aftermath of that, and hormonal changes, but Chris had been there, had seen it all happen, and was Ben's father and my husband. Why should he not be just as much affected as I was? The British stiff upper lip can be a menace! The doctor also gave me some sleeping pills, but I was not keen, not wanting to get into any cycle of dependency on medication to survive.

That evening I rang my good friend Pauline (who had lost her first baby two years before), and she was really helpful. What she said arose from her own experience, but had been carefully processed over time. It was strangely comforting to be told we would never 'get over it'; already we knew that Ben's birth had changed our lives, and we did not want things to go back to normal as if he had never been born. She encouraged us to try to think of all the positive things we could connected with Ben's life; this was going to be hard because it was so short, so we would have to think about the eight months I carried him as well. Then she talked about the importance of sharing and grieving with Chris as much as possible; her comments would become a salutary reminder in the weeks to come. Finally she said we should try to remember that her daughter, Alex, and our son, Ben, would have chosen God as their father before us as their parents if they had had the choice. I could accept this because it came from someone who knew, but I also found it rather hard to own for myself. My mind was doing its Christian duty, but my heart was not so sure.

Our local undertaker came to talk about funeral arrangements; he was a friend, and was terribly upset himself, because he had grandchildren the same age as Sarah. We had every confidence in him; he offered to make a coffin when I said how much I disliked the customized white boxes that seem to be the norm for children's funerals (and when it came to the funeral, he carried it in the most natural way, tucked under his arm); we gave him a little hand-embroidered nightdress my cousin had given us for Ben, which we asked that he be dressed in. We had decided on cremation rather than burial because we knew that one day we would move away from Hawes (Methodist ministers normally stay for five years in one place, and then move on), and we did not want to leave a little grave behind. We were fortunate in managing to get a slot booked at the crematorium before Christmas, so the date was set for 22 December.

There was a sense of timelessness about the next few days. People came and went; Chris and Sarah went to Northallerton to register Ben's birth and death. This seemed to take for ever as they had to wait to get the death certificate signed at the hospital because the doctor was asleep after a long night. We didn't begrudge her the rest, but it was just one thing more to cope with. The registrar then upset Chris by looking at Sarah and saying that we could always have another, which seemed to dismiss what had happened. Neither of us was sleeping well, and we talked in the small hours of the morning when we realized that we were both awake. So much for the doctor's pills, but it was time well spent. The days were full of visitors, and the house was full of family, which was good on one level (Sarah was never bored), but I had a longing for space. We badly needed to touch base with each other; 3 a.m. seemed to be a good time.

The tragedy of the terrorist bomb on Pan Am flight 103 over Lockerbie happened just a few days later, on 21 December, and the entire nation was thrown into shock and mourning. My diary entry reflects the turmoil: *How can we deal with our personal loss in the context of the death of hundreds of innocent people, just a few miles away?* My mother and brother had to drive down from Edinburgh for the funeral through all the debris. The immediate effect on me was to think that the loss of our newborn child simply would no longer feature on the agendas of other people, because it had been eclipsed by a far bigger tragedy. Of course, his death dominated *my* whole being, but I questioned how right this was. There is a biblical text, Ecclesiastes 6.3–5, which seems to deny significance to a stillborn child:

> A man may beget a hundred children, and live for many years; but however many are the days of his years, if he does not enjoy life's good things, or has no burial, I say that a stillborn child is better off than he. For it comes into vanity and goes into darkness, and in darkness its name is covered; moreover it has not seen the sun or known anything; yet it finds rest rather than he.

How significant was any life, anyway? What was it all about? Psalm 39.4b–5 asks a similar question:

Let me know how fleeting my life is.
You have made my days a few handbreadths,
and my lifetime is as nothing in your sight.

Jessica's poetry picks up the same theme:

> Your life was just a fingerprint
> on the glass of eternity
> soon to be washed off
> and disappear.

How could a baby, who had lived barely an hour, fill our hearts and minds, when thousands of people were mourning the loss of husbands, wives, parents, children and friends? And how dare we want, or expect, understanding and sympathy from people near us, if Ben had actually paled into insignificance beside the crash? If our friends and family did actually appear to care, were they not doing it just out of love and kindness, when in reality they were rather impatient with our grief and wishing we could get it into proportion? These were thoughts that were running through my mind, which I barely mentioned to anyone else, and which were probably quite unjustified. Expectations had quickly begun to play a part, in this case my expectations of others, and these were actually coloured by my own unresolved questions; these in turn gave rise to feelings of guilt and inadequacy. Grief can be very complex, because of the huge mix of emotions involved.

> Oh death,
> where is thy sting?
> they ask, who do not know;
> I'll tell you where it is,
> it's in the heart of me,
> thrashing and stinging,
> where only love should be.

There was a lovely elderly lady in our congregation in Hawes, well into her eighties, who made a point of coming to see me. She wanted to tell me about the stillborn child she had had at home, over 60 years before, who had been taken away from her at birth, wrapped in newspaper, and put out with the rubbish. She needed to talk, because she had not been allowed to grieve at the time. She had been expected to get on with her life as if nothing had happened. She also wanted to reassure me that our child had mattered, and that we needed to be allowed to grieve.

An opportune visit from our friend, Clare Anderson, helped enormously. I was nervous of meeting her again, acutely aware that she had lost her adult son in particularly tragic circumstances, in July 1976. We rarely spoke of him directly when we visited them; I had some hazy details from my aunt, who was a personal friend, but I had always had the feeling that this was hallowed ground on which I did not wish to tread. This is how she told the story to me for the purpose of this book:

> From the age of four to five, Robin suffered from major epileptic attacks. He and I were flown to Hong Kong from Taiwan, where the family lived, for treatment at Queen Mary's Hospital. The seizures were brought under control; later, in England, he was under the care of Great Ormond Street Hospital for children from the age of 8 to 15, when he was finally taken off the medication. All this affected his life at school, but he had many interests: archaeology, work for Amnesty International, the writing of stories and poems, history, prolific reading. He was sociable, humorous, courageous and philosophical about his difficulties beyond his age.
>
> When he left school at the age of 17 he put into practice his concern for and strong views on injustice, disadvantage and poverty, first

working in a voluntary capacity with mentally challenged young adults in Lancashire and then, with the Cyrenians, in hostels for homeless men in Rochester and Swansea. At this time he was a member of the Peace Pledge Union and as such became seriously involved in issues such as Northern Ireland. It was just after doing a job for this that he met his death: he wandered too far out on the sands at Llanelli and was caught by the tide coming in and swept out to sea.

Robin was a lifelong Christian; he died with a cross of Welsh slate around his neck which he wore under his shirt. And there it remained. He was 21 and had been accepted for training as a social worker at the Selly Oak Colleges in Birmingham that autumn. He was greatly looking forward to it.

At the time, I had only a vague picture in my mind of what had happened; the details emerged over the years. But it was enough to be aware of the outline, and to see the impact this loss had had on her life. How could I look her in the face, devastated as I was by our own loss? She tackled the problem head on, asserting with heartfelt conviction that I should not even try to compare griefs. Each is complete and overwhelming in itself, and it is right that it should be. She cried with me, and restored the sense that we were actually entitled to grieve; not to do so would be to deny Ben. This gave us the courage to go ahead with the funeral; we had not actually considered changing our plans, but had been feeling rather uneasy about having a service for everyone in view of the nation's grief.

Here, even here
a rope reaches down
friends, known and unknown
bend down in love
to help me out.

Meanwhile, we continued to be overwhelmed by people's kindness, and the house looked like Kew Gardens, with poinsettias on every possible shelf and windowsill, even on the landing. Ever since then I have not been overfond of that plant! One arrangement arrived with a florist's label on it for 'the late Ben Paul Shreeve', and that nearly finished me off. It seemed such an inappropriate thing to write.

In some ways, the funeral was reminiscent of our wedding; we had thought hard, if swiftly, about what we wanted, choosing the hymns, readings and music, but when it came to the actual event, it almost washed over us. We were very aware of the pain that our families were suffering, and sensed that much of this was on our behalf; they were trying to imagine how we must be feeling, and experiencing that as well as their own grief, which must have been strange as they were mourning a child they had never seen. Chris's mother, we knew, was devastated at the loss of her first grandson, having so far been presented with four granddaughters, and although gender simply was not an issue for us, we had to accept that it appeared more important to her. Both mothers were doubtless also experiencing the pain that comes simply with being a parent and watching a child suffer, compounded by being widows; we had moved a long way from a kiss and a piece of sticking plaster applied to the wound bringing instant recovery.

An old friend of the family, Professor Kingsley Barrett, kindly agreed to speak at the service; he had accompanied me down the aisle at our wedding, my father having died the previous year, and now we were asking him to do a very difficult thing. He did not let us down, and what he said helped us continue in the days that followed:

'I shall go to him, but he will not return to me'
(2 Samuel 12.23).

We are here because Esther and Chris wish us to share in their gratitude for the gift of Ben Paul and for the privilege of loving and caring for him for an hour – No! Of caring for him for an hour, and loving him for ever.

We are not the only ones to care and love. In the words we have just heard (John 14.1–6, 27), St John reminds us that in the Father's house there are many mansions – many rooms, as the translation in the service book has it; and we may be certain that among the rooms there is a nursery, where the Lord himself welcomes and looks after his little ones. That is not romantic and sentimental imagination, for here, having heard St John, we may call St Mark to our aid, as he tells us (Mark 10.13–16) of the Lord's indignation when people tried to keep him and the children apart. And what he was once, he is for ever.

When his little son was grievously ill, King David lay on his bed in such an anguish of distress and prayer that his servants hardly dared to tell him of the boy's death, and they were astounded when he got up, washed and changed, and returned to the business of life. No, he said; while he lived I could pray. Now I shall go to him, but he will not come to me (2 Samuel 12.23). There is rationality in that; and reason is not a bad thing. It can steady our emotions and give us poise. Still more, there is great courage in it; and courage is a supremely good thing. You cannot get through the hard places of life without it.

But there is something else, which David could only begin to articulate. 'I shall go to him.' But shall I? Is there any means by which we can share the destiny of still untouched, unclouded innocence? There is, though to find it we are driven back to unplumbed depths. David could pray for it: 'Have mercy upon me, O God, according to thy loving kindness: according unto the multitude of thy tender mercies, blot out my transgressions.' And the New Testament affirms it: 'If we walk in the light, as he is in the light, we have fellowship with one another, and the blood of Jesus Christ, God's Son, cleanseth us from all sin.' There, by the mercy of God, even we can be one with the innocents, where all families are united, and all families are one.

We are thankful for a brief hour in the past, and for all whose love and care and skill contributed to it; and we are thankful for a future, hidden now in the mystery of God's own love and care and wisdom.

It was good to be sent a copy of his address a week or so later, so that we could read it at our leisure, and take in what he had said, because that simply had not been possible during the service. Afterwards, we wished we had asked the undertaker to arrange a way of providing a list of the people who came to the funeral; the church seemed very full, but the faces were all a blur, and we left straightaway to drive to the crematorium. We knew that some very good friends had not come, but they had taken care to explain that this was because they did not feel they could cope with the service, and were struggling themselves. Some of these were not Christian.

The journey up to the crematorium in Darlington was memorable; only the family and Kingsley and Margaret Barrett came to that, so we were a small line of private cars. My mother, whose driving had often given us cause for concern, nearly went under a juggernaut as she emerged from the slip road on to the A1. We saw it in the mirror, and could do nothing! Let this be a lesson to us not to allow anyone to drive when under stress; we chose to go in our own cars because we thought it was less pretentious, and it would have cost so much to hire, but we really shouldn't have let her drive.

> Today, as weeping,
> I drove home
> from shopping
> as I have done
> so often
> since he died,
> I thought to myself;
> can they prosecute you
> for driving whilst under
> the influence of emotion?

There was a moment of near hysteria as we entered the crematorium chapel, because the piped music that was laid on started playing Brahms' *Lullaby*. I nearly choked with laughter after I had got over the shock – it simply hadn't occurred to us to specify 'no music, please'. Chris was supposedly the professional at this, but it had not dawned on him either. My family was particularly outraged, I guess because it was a much loved and played piece of music in our home, and it just did not feel appropriate for this occasion. After a few bars we managed to have it turned off. My brother-in-law, James (who is also a Methodist minister – we have a few of them in my family!), did the committal, with the lovely words of John Henry Newman, which we had asked him to read:

Go forth upon your journey, Christian soul,
In the name of God the Father
who created you;
In the name of Jesus Christ,
who suffered for you;
In the name of the Holy Spirit,
who strengthens you;
In communion with the blessed saints,
With angels, archangels
and with all the heavenly host.
May you rest in peace
And may the City of God
Be your eternal dwelling. Amen.

(*Methodist Worship Book*, p. 431)

The funeral was a milestone; I had been concerned about getting through the day without breaking down, so had agreed to take a tranquillizer, which had the desired effect. The doctor had also given me some medication to stop my milk coming in. Although it was good not to be leaking everywhere, the net result was that I felt very uncomfortable, and being on the receiving end of the many hugs that were given to me that day was rather painful – just a counter-irritation to keep me on my toes.

That evening we all sat and watched *The Sound of Music*. Chris had never seen it. His brother, Paul, cracked very funny and cynical asides all the way through, which broke the tension beautifully. Laughter is therapeutic, and this was the first time we had laughed for nearly a week. It took us by surprise, but we were grateful to find that we could have moments of enjoyment, and did not feel guilty about them. I don't think I will ever see that film in the same light again. Sarah then proceeded to put a spanner in the works by coming down with chickenpox; we had thought she was cross because of the tensions in the family around the funeral, but the doctor noticed the spots and diagnosed it straightaway when he came to check up on us. This was another blessing in disguise; after the busyness of Christmas, it gave me an excuse to pull up the drawbridge for a few days, and keep a low profile.

A few days remained before Christmas. Chris resumed his normal duties, with the round of carol services and other festivities keeping him busy; we made a point of walking into town together one day to do some last bits of shopping, and going into all the shops, so that the ice was broken. I wanted to feel I had seen as many people as possible, and given them a chance to say what they wanted to say, in the hope of finding a new kind of normality after the Christmas period. We were prepared for people avoiding us, perhaps even crossing the road to get out of our way, but that never happened in Hawes. This is the advantage of living in a small community where everyone knows everyone else, and it seems the most natural thing to want to express human concern. Personally, I much prefer that to the anonymity of living in a suburb, where it can feel as though people are terrified of showing their vulnerability or humanity.

Why can't Christmas always be on a Sunday, as it was that year? It makes life so much more manageable for a clergy family. I love it every time it happens, which is all too rarely; to have Christmas Eve services on Saturday evening leading on to the celebrations of Christmas Day feels so tidy, and a good use of time! My worst-case scenario is when Christmas falls on a Saturday, and one is left with the anti-climax of Sunday and empty churches.

Chris took all the services he was scheduled to take, apart from the united service at the Parish Church, which included a baptism – the vicar told him not to come. He and his wife had lost a baby too, so we knew they understood. I went to a midnight service, taking advantage of having live-in babysitters, and then the evening one at Hawes, to support Chris. The day proceeded in a very comfortable way; I would not have believed it possible to have so many people participating in the cooking of a turkey without coming to blows, but the atmosphere in the kitchen was very relaxed and convivial. We have never subscribed to the commercialization of Christmas anyway, preferring to keep it quiet and simple, but somehow the meaning was very clear and poignant that year. God sent his Son. We had begun to understand that in a different light.

After Christmas, all the family went home, and we were on our own for the first time. We felt rather as if we were in limbo; traditionally, the week between Christmas and New Year is a quiet one for Chris, and we had craved the space, but we actually found it quite hard to deal with when we got it. Sarah was very bored as a result. She wasn't particularly ill, but we could not go out, except for walks, and the weather was not particularly conducive to spending much time outside. One walks slowly with a toddler, and it was cold! I felt increasingly low and can remember vividly one evening.

I cried in the bath. Ben so enjoyed baths; that was when he seemed to be most lively and I missed his squirming and kicking. I wonder if he squirmed more because he had 12 fingers and toes? As I cried, I leaked milk – it seemed as if my whole body was weeping. The feeling of physical emptiness was quite overwhelming, and yet I was grateful for it. Chris observed that at least I had had Ben for eight months; he only held him for half an hour.

As soon as Sarah's spots began to heal, we took ourselves off for a day in York and bought Sarah a proper xylophone. We seemed to have a creative urge, and Chris was keen to make her a doll's pram, so we spent ages choosing the wood and the paint for it. Retail therapy? Quite possibly, but it was good to get out and breathe. We had an entertaining time when we went for lunch at a pizzeria, spending some of our Christmas money; we were in a little booth, enjoying our meal, when Sarah stood up and looked over the partition at the next family. They were obviously concerned because of her spotty face; we had a clear conscience because the doctor had told us we could go, but they were not to know that. It was another moment of humour for us, and we needed every one we could get.

As 1988 drew to a close, I wondered what the new one would bring.

I had no feeling of anticipation as I opened the new calendar, simply a reminder that he had been due on 12 January, and nothing now is going to happen. 1988 was Ben's year, and I guess we will always think of it that way. Instead of going to the usual New Year's Eve party, a meal on wheels was delivered by our friends with love, which was very touching. It was a wonderful feast, with all sorts of tempting treats, and we felt a bit guilty as we ate it – are you meant to enjoy food when you have just lost a baby?

Mostly we didn't: 'For I eat ashes like bread, and mingle tears with my drink' (Psalm 102.9), but this was an exception, typical of the roller coaster of grief.

Early in January we took Sarah in the car, and scattered Ben's ashes at our favourite picnic spot in Dentdale, a few miles from Hawes. Doing it this way meant we could always return to our special place, and not worry about upkeep and maintenance, and this has indeed proved to be the case. Whenever we are in the area, we try to visit Ben's valley, as we have come to call it. We felt like limp lettuce afterwards, but that was only to be expected. It felt as if the first phase in our journey was drawing to a close. When we moved house a few years later, we decided to plant a rose in his memory in our new garden, because it would be hard to visit Dentdale regularly; interestingly, when we came to move on from there, eight years later, we felt no particular need to transplant it, perhaps because by then we had established our own pattern for remembering him, which we knew included regular, if infrequent, visits to his valley, so did not need to take the rose bush with us. But at the time we could not know how we were going to work through our grief and deal with our memories.

4

Back to Normal?

Do you want to see my scream?
I'll open my mouth
and you will see it
if you look.

Just as a child
opens their mouth
and places the tip of their finger
to show you the place
and says,
'Do you want to see my wobbly tooth?'
so I wonder,
if you look down my throat,
is the scream there for you to see?

And, if I look down your throat,
is there a scream down there
too?

The next few months were hard work. It was the
dead time of year, and although I cannot remember
much about the weather, I have an overall impression
of darkness, greyness and cold. The new normality we
thought we should be striving towards was elusive.
We continued to be walking through uncharted
territory, and we seemed be involved in a variety of
circumstances which were beyond our control, which
added to our feelings of confusion.

The day after we had scattered Ben's ashes we
returned to the Friarage Hospital to see our
consultant and to have blood tests for chromosome
testing. He was able to tell us some more about

Trisomy 13 (often known as Patau's syndrome), which was useful. Only one in every 12,000 live births is affected; many babies with the condition are in fact spontaneously aborted at an earlier stage in the pregnancy. Just because we had had one child born with the condition, there was no reason to fear it could happen to us again, although the older the mother is, the more chance there is of something untoward happening. He was very reassuring about our chances of having a normal baby when the time was right, but counselled against us trying to conceive again immediately, which I sometimes felt I wanted to do; the feeling of emptiness could be absolutely overwhelming, and it was very tempting to want to change it. Chris was much more cautious. But we were agreed that we should wait until the genetic tests came back, so that we could make an informed decision about the future. He was delighted with the cheque we gave him for the Special Care Baby Unit, which came partly from donations at the funeral, and partly from us – it seemed little enough to us, but he seemed almost overcome. When we thought of how much money we would have had to find to be able to care for Ben ourselves, or to travel to see him wherever he had been cared for, we felt that what we gave was a drop in the ocean.

The next excitement was Chris coming down with full-blown, proper, flu. This was a classic example of how grief takes its physical toll; our immune systems were not doing what they should have done because we were struggling with the bereavement. I wasn't feeling too well either, but before I succumbed I offered to take the Covenant Service at Hawes. I knew what an important service this is for many Methodists; it is an opportunity to commit oneself again to God, for whatever the new year holds, and I hated to think that it would have to be delayed for another six weeks or so, which would be the earliest date that Chris could be at that chapel again. There is a set order of service, which I knew I could lead easily; the congregation would have to do without Communion, and there would only be a very short sermon. But I was very anxious to say something, and that particular service provided me with what I considered an excellent context to say it. So many people had said to us that we had lost Ben so that we would be better equipped for ministry in the future, this would enrich our lives, etc. This incensed me, because it conjured up a picture of an idiosyncratic, wilful God, who pushes a button on the computer keyboard to send a spot of suffering down on to some hapless human being to make them a better person – one kind of interpretation of Psalm 115.3: 'Our God is in the heavens; he does whatever he pleases.' I needed to put the record straight, so I took as my text the Covenant Prayer, and in particular the first few lines:

> I am no longer my own, but yours.
> Put me to what you will,
> Rank me with whom you will;
> Put me to doing,
> Put me to suffering ...

> (*Methodist Worship Book*, p. 290)

I could not, and would not, believe for an instant that the God of steadfast love (Psalm 136), in whom I had always believed, could want to inflict pain on any of his children. The picture of Jesus weeping by Lazarus' tomb (John 11.34) meant everything. Yes, terrible things happen, and through them, somehow, God can be glorified, but that is not *why* they occur. I think I ended my very brief homily with a reference to 1 Corinthians 13.12: 'For now we see in a mirror dimly, but then we will see face to face. Now I know only in part; then I will know fully, even as I have been fully known.' This was probably the shortest, and most vehement, sermon I have ever preached. With hindsight I would question the advisability of doing it, because I was still so raw and vulnerable, but no one complained – and it was the beginning of my own call to become a preacher.

I might have dismissed the idea that God had inflicted this experience of suffering on us to make us more caring and sensitive people, but something lingered and did have an effect on me. Over the next few years, whenever there was a late miscarriage, or cot death, or similar tragedy in the community, I identified strongly with the family, and particularly the mother, whom I was quite likely to know anyway. I thought I was being helpful, and I was sure that I knew the right things to say and what not to say – but I could not see that my concerns were rooted in my own pain and needs. I hope I had enough sensitivity to know when I was welcome, and when I was regarded as a nuisance. As the minister's wife, it was simply accepted that I would have a pastoral concern in this kind of situation, and no one ever suggested to me that it might be inappropriate for me to visit. In fact, they were much more likely to approve, believing that I, if anyone, would be able to empathize. Certainly, Chris's ministry was appreciated. When he went to see one family after the cot death of their son, he admitted to them that he had no words, or answers. They replied that that was exactly why they wanted him there: 'You understand,' they said.

My hesitation today about my feelings and actions in those situations stems from the counselling training I did later and the lessons I learned about the importance of being properly debriefed before supporting people who are in any kind of need which may have echoes of one's own story. I had in fact experienced the dangers myself; one day (before we had started bereavement counselling) when I was feeling particularly low, I rang a local helpline for people in my situation, and spoke to someone who proceeded to recount her own story at great length, and barely listened to me. This should have been a salutary lesson, but it was several years before I made the connection.

Immediately after my foray into the pulpit I too got flu. I joined Chris in bed, where we overlapped for about three days, and were bailed out by my mother and her cousin, who looked after us superbly. Brenda was sensitive to our state of health and mind and introduced us to the *Brother Cadfael* novels by Ellis Peters, which made excellent convalescent reading. There is nothing wrong with escapism, and we were pleased to discover a good author who was new to us both.

Once I had recovered, there seemed no reason to prevent me picking up the threads of 'normal' life again, not that it felt anything like normal, of course. I was still in a fog, but was determined to go through the motions of everyday life, in the hope that one day it would feel right again. Ben's due date came and went, and was very difficult to deal with:

It seems like years since he was born, and yet like only yesterday, and every day that passes serves only to increase the divide between us. I desperately do not want his memory to fade, and ask myself again and again why I did not hold him for longer, and why couldn't I bring myself to look at his hands and feet?

In my misery, I felt that somehow I had let him down. Each day seemed like an eternity at this stage; everything was such hard work. I wanted to cope, and to be seen to be coping; what was the point of being a Christian if one could not demonstrate the power of faith, and the difference that it makes? 'My tears have been my food day and night, while people say to me continually, "Where is your God?"' (Psalm 42.3). Not that anyone ever challenged me, but I was acutely aware of how I must be presenting myself to friends and neighbours who had no faith. Surely belief in the resurrection should transform the experience of grieving?

Our Christmas cards had been addressed and ready to send before Ben's arrival; they went into the wastepaper collection, and we hastily sent out a newsletter to all our friends, telling them what had happened. It was very upbeat:

> Spiritually, we have been tremendously encouraged by the loving support of family, friends, and the community. In no way do we mourn helplessly, as we know Ben is now complete in heaven, surrounded by the perfect love of our Father. Our parental love is but a poor imitation.

The letter reached many more people than we had expected or intended. During and after his service in the Royal Air Force, Chris had been a member of the Officers' Christian Union (for all military services). Parts of our newsletter were reproduced in the Officers' Christian Union newsletter in February; we had no objection, but were surprised and moved to receive various letters from members of the OCU in the following weeks.

Putting a brave face on it was relatively easy when writing a letter; day-to-day life and conversation were more of a challenge. I nearly hit a well-meaning companion who said, 'But you know your treasure is in heaven', in an attempt to offer comfort. It sounded like a hollow cliché which did nothing whatsoever to help; I fumed about it for weeks afterwards, in something of the same way Job must have done (Job

16.3). And yet it was simply another expression of what we had written in our own letter! Friends and relations had to tread very carefully when they were with me, because it was so difficult to strike the right chord; what I knew, and what I felt, were quite contradictory, so how could anyone possibly guess how to approach me?

> I'm walking on eggshells
> into the future,
> taking each day
> a task at a time;
> and not looking back,
> and not looking forward,
> for behind is only loss,
> and ahead is the unknown.
>
> Sometimes I can grasp
> the gift of the day,
> and hold it as such
> with my being,
> but at other times
> the tide rises
> and the misery surfaces
> once again.

With some hesitation, I braved the toddler group at church for the first time, helped by a friend who came to hold my hand. I made myself hold a baby boy, who had been born two weeks before Ben, and found that I actually enjoyed cuddling him; but it was something of an ordeal, knowing that I was being watched. On another occasion, two or three months after Ben had died, a young mother was there who had had a baby around the same time.

Her daughter was sitting, propped up by cushions, and taking notice; I caught her eye and the mother said, 'Wouldn't you just love to have one like this?' I wanted the floor to open and swallow me up; I simply did not know where to put myself or what to do, but managed to hold out for a few minutes, talking about something or nothing to the person sitting next to me, before I made a bolt for the vestry and sobbed.

I wonder if she ever realized what she had said or what its effect had been. But we all say tactless and hurtful things, and this was just a spectacular instance.

I see the world through my loss
everything that happens
I see in that way.

The world may see me smile
and answer rationally
but inside my mind
I'm thinking of you.

I may be speaking lightly
of interesting things
but everything I say
is tinged with you.

I may be singing hymns
apparently devout
but the lines and the words
remind me of you.

I may be making plans
but they are not real
I'm just pretending
because I live in the past
where you lived with me.

The past is my future
gone and gone again
and the future is my past.

We knew we had to face the future and tried to move on in hope. With some trepidation we acquired a puppy; we had talked about this before Ben was born, and had decided that it would be nice to have a family dog as well as our two cats. My sister, Ruth, knew our plans, and suggested that we should go ahead; she went to the Animal Rescue Shelter near her home and reported that she had found a very promising three-month-old abandoned mongrel, a cross between a collie and a spaniel. She had tested the dog out on her own very young children, and she had passed with flying colours. I was quite keen, being an animal-minded person, but Chris was more hesitant; we talked it over for a couple of days before we decided to go ahead.

So Mop joined the family, originally christened because the name was easy for Sarah to say; however, we swiftly discovered how particularly appropriate it was, because she was not at all well. At first we attributed it to carsickness and stress from the journey, but after a few days we realized that there was something more serious afoot. A highly stressful time followed; because she was ill, she could not have her injections, so could not be taken out for walks; although she was semi-house-trained, the nature of her upset digestive system meant that there were many accidents, and our two cats were absolutely outraged, retreating behind the stairgate, and making upstairs their territory. One memorable Sunday evening, when Chris had just gone out to take a service, the dog had an attack of diarrhoea at the front door, and Sarah, who had had a bath and was in a clean sleepsuit, paraded through the mess. I didn't know who or what to deal with first.

Mop continued for some weeks to be a constant worry; her stomach problems simply would not go away, and we were regular visitors to the vet. The garden was not fenced, and the house was on a busy trans-Pennine route, so we had to spend what felt like endless, freezing hours in the garden with her. During the dark evenings, that was no picnic. Finally, as a last resort, the vet suggested that we wean her again, with a teaspoon of food every hour or so, and that did the trick. We had also worked out that she could not tolerate tinned food; once we got her diet sorted, all was well, and early in March we took her out in triumph for her first proper walk. From that point, she was a real joy to the family, and was with us for another 15 years. But the uncertainty about her future, and the real fear that we would have to have her put to sleep, was an extra pressure on us for a couple of months, not aided by the fact that Chris had been less than keen at the outset to embark on a puppy at that stage. However, he never once said 'I told you so', and grew to love her as much as everyone else; even the cats were quickly won over, and often shared her basket.

I was struggling, but did not want to interrupt Chris in his work. There was a big part of me that needed him to be on top of things, getting on with the huge pile of outstanding jobs that awaited him, and I feared that my unhappiness would hold him back. He had always been my rock – calm, placid, stable, reassuring, but now I needed him to grieve with me in a demonstrable way, so that I could be reassured that I was not on my own in my misery. He did not find that easy, caught between wanting to be strong for me, and not being very good at showing his vulnerability anyway. Sarah required our attention, time and energy, and I quickly ran out of patience and energy when it came to dealing with a busy toddler. Chris was much better in that department, and took her with him as often as he could; every Tuesday afternoon she would go with him to Thornton Lodge, the local small hospital for people with learning difficulties, where he was chaplain. That gave me space for myself (and the opportunity for a nap!) but made me feel guilty as well – why couldn't I be a super-competent mother, who could look after her child and make no extra demands of her husband?

These were my complexes, even hang-ups; Chris was coming at things from a completely different perspective. But our expectations of ourselves and of each other remained unspoken. I discovered years later that he felt I was trying to do too much too soon; that he wanted me to know that I came first, before the demands of ministry, and that he was more than pleased to play his part in looking after Sarah. The knowledge that the Yorkshire farmers whom he met daily looked askance at him when they met him pushing the pram through town, or admitted to changing nappies, did not worry him in the least. His youngest brother, David, was ten years younger, and he had been used to helping out with him at home. As a result he was very happy and natural in the role of childminder, nappies and all.

I was much more concerned than he was that he should be accepted and respected as a 'good minister', and did not want to do anything that might compromise that. This was where bereavement counselling would come into its own because it facilitated open, honest and risky conversations. In mid-January we had an appointment to meet our counsellor, but I had to work hard to persuade Chris to come with me. Neither of us had ever had counselling before, and fear of the unknown certainly played a part in his hesitation, but so too did a degree of suspicion about sharing his deep personal feelings with a stranger, and worry about being perceived as failing in some way. It is interesting to note that the start of counselling did not signal an immediate improvement in our relationship; in fact, things were going to get a lot worse before they began to improve. Fortunately, we were not blessed with the ability to see into the future.

5

Grieving Separately, Together

Hilary, our bereavement counsellor, might have been tailor-made for us. In fact, she was the answer to the prayers that had been said on our behalf. She is a daughter of an Anglican priest, so she understood much of our situation instinctively, without us having to spell it out. Our first meeting with her was very much a 'getting to know you' kind of affair, and we were relieved to discover that she was not at all concerned when we turned up with Sarah, whose presence provided light relief. It transpired that she had young children herself, and had lost her husband two years before, but she was very careful not to talk about herself, other than to put us at our ease. She was one of the few people we could talk to about Ben as a person in his own right, in a way that was not contrived or artificial. We were hampered in this because we were the only people who had seen him and held him; we had a photograph that we shared with our close family and friends, but it was not the same! Nothing quite compensates for shared experience. Hilary, a midwife, was working with the people who had looked after us on the night Ben was born; she had heard them talk about him which gave her a link to him, and that was reassuring for us.

It was providential that we had already made contact with Hilary before Sarah became a cause of real concern with her recurring ear infections. This came to a head at the beginning of February when she ran a temperature of over 104° late one Sunday night.

*We rang the doctor, who came straightaway,
took one look, and told us to get into the car
and go to the hospital, and not to wait for the
ambulance. As he rang the hospital, telling the
children's ward that a recently bereaved
family was on its way in with a very sick child,
he was nearly in tears himself, which we found
both touching, and alarming. That drive was a
nightmare; I sat in the back with Sarah on my
knee, while Chris drove faster than he had ever
done before (or since!); I realized that I was
beyond prayer, other than shouting at God
that enough was enough.*

Rouse yourself! Why do you sleep,
O Lord?
Awake, do not cast us off for ever!
Why do you hide your face?
Why do you forget our affliction and
        oppression?

(Psalm 44.23–24)

We were admitted straight on to the children's
ward, and Sarah was examined, given various
medications, stripped to her nappy, and put under a
fan. We were then horrified to have another
paediatrician arrive and examine her closely for signs
of abuse – this was shortly after the Cleveland child
abuse scandal, and we discovered later that it was
routine procedure for every new admission, but it was
a shock at the time.

Chris left the hospital at 2 a.m., and Sarah and I
stayed on the ward together for three long days. This
was one of our lowest points; once her temperature
was under control the agonizing worry receded, but
we had to see various doctors about her ears, and
wait to get the all-clear to go home. Chris commuted
back and forth, putting the dog in the garage for the
four hours he had to allow for the journey and a

decent visit. I scarcely slept as I had a camp bed beside Sarah's cot; she didn't like the cot and could only be persuaded to sleep if she got into bed with me. Mercifully we had a room to ourselves. It was heartbreaking to observe the comings and goings on the ward; a child was dying in the room next to us, and the staff were, of course, preoccupied. I didn't begrudge the family their attention for a moment, but it was a scenario I found very difficult to be near.

All I wanted was to be told we could go home – and the doctors were too busy. I felt trapped, and isolated; the presence of Hilary upstairs on the maternity ward saved my sanity – I could nip up to see her for odd minutes when Sarah was asleep. Just knowing that there was someone in the building who understood what we were going through made it possible to survive those days of being cut off from the rest of the world, locked into a routine and system over which we had no control. It was another situation, like Lockerbie, in which I felt caught by comparing griefs; there was a family in the room next to us, devastated by the death of their child who had lived, and had a real life, whom they had known and loved, who had a personality, and friends; and there was me, with one moderately poorly toddler who was on the road to recovery, grieving for a newborn infant who had died six weeks before. How dared I feel as wretched as I was? Hilary listened, and empathized, and made me feel that my misery was valid and understandable – even necessary, if I was going to get through.

After that interlude, an appointment was made for Sarah to see an ear, nose and throat consultant which came through very quickly. A hearing test was done and she was found to be about 50 per cent deaf, which stunned us as her speech appeared to be coming on very well. We agreed that she should be put on the waiting list for grommets to be inserted, and meanwhile tried to find alternative ways of keeping her as healthy as possible; by this time she had had so many antibiotics, she rattled. I was also lurching from throat infection to infection, and Chris was in a state of constant exhaustion. A friend put us on to a homeopath/naturopath in Newcastle whom we went to see at the end of February. The treatment was not cheap, nor was the healthy living regime she recommended to us, but we felt it was money well spent, and it meant a precious day out as a family. Days off at home never seemed particularly successful, because we were too available. Sarah was very amenable to days of only eating fruit and vegetables; we cut down drastically on dairy produce whenever any of us had colds, and it did seem to help, over a period of time. One of the key things was feeling that at last we were able to do something to help ourselves, and take control. That was worth a lot.

In addition to advice she gave us about diet, and the homeopathic medication, our naturopath talked with us about a future pregnancy. I had just had to go through my postnatal check, which had felt like the final insult. It is never a pleasant experience, but to have to go through it when there is no baby waiting for you at home, is an ordeal which simply has to be endured. These were early days, but I knew I needed reassurance that we could go ahead and try again. Once the results of the blood tests had come through, which they did in the middle of February, we knew for sure, as the consultant had already surmised, that there was no genetic reason not to try again. But the naturopath counselled caution, suggesting that we should wait a year before we tried, to give my body time to return to normal, and to allow ourselves time to grieve, so that another baby would not be seen as a substitute for Ben. I had had two pregnancies in quick succession, and these had taken their toll.

This was something I really did not want to hear, but I could see the sense of what she was saying. Chris's response was rather different. He was already concerned about his age, and was very fearful of what another pregnancy might do to me. We began to think about the possibility of adoption, because we agreed that we did not want Sarah be an only child. Both of us have siblings, and we had always imagined that we would have at least two children, if not more. But we were worried about how other people might respond to us having an adopted child, or children, and perhaps treating them differently from Sarah. One of the problems of telling our families and friends about our genetic tests was that they all knew we had the 'all clear', and we sensed that some might not understand why we had therefore decided to go down the adoption route. How far was this decision going to be our own, and how far were we going to be swayed by the unspoken assumptions and expectations of others? In the end, we let it rest for several months, and only spoke of it intermittently; when the year was up, we had (with the help of Hilary) come to a common mind that we would try for another baby, and see what happened.

We were grieving differently, and separately, which was hard. My friend Pauline had warned us that this might happen; I think I had had in mind those people whom one reads about (I was doing a lot of reading) who said that a particular tragedy had brought them together. For us it felt quite the opposite and we struggled with guilt because there seemed to be a high and impenetrable brick wall between us. On one occasion we stood in opposite corners of our very large kitchen, almost like boxers in a ring, desperate to communicate, hoping for a response from each other, and getting nowhere – fast.

It was as if an abyss had opened at our feet, and somehow we have to hang on to one another to stop ourselves from toppling into it. How can two people who care so much for each other, and who have so much in common, not least the shared loss of a child, find it so appallingly difficult to express their feelings? Why can't we understand each other's pain, and how it is affecting us?

The pain is snarling in my soul,
twisting the very body of me
into screaming knots.
It is eating away my being
corrupting the image of You
in me
so that I am becoming
nothing at all
just pain.

Is this what it felt like to You
as you hung on the tree
in silence and agony?
Did the horror of our sin
our heaped corruption piled
on You
mean that you became
nothing at all
just pain?

Lord, I know that the pain I have
is just a pale reflection
of what You chose to bear,
and that others have much
greater burdens
than I;
but I have had enough, Lord,
and I can take
no more.

We were frightened by the sheer power of the emotions we were feeling, which we could not describe or share. This was a shock in itself, as we are both articulate individuals who normally manage to communicate quite easily! One of the main differences between the ways Chris and I viewed things was that I was grieving for the baby who had died; Chris focused more on his handicaps, and was relieved he hadn't lived. We managed to talk about this one evening as we drove home from a visit to Newcastle; Sarah was asleep in the back of the car, and the fact that we were driving made the conversation less threatening and confrontational than in a face-to-face situation, such as the one we had had in the kitchen. It was a matter of emphasis, not of different standpoints. Of course I was aware that, had Ben lived, our lives would have been completely turned upside down as we got used to having a member of the family who needed full-time care. But my empty arms still physically ached to hold him, I still felt his movements inside me (is this reminiscent of what amputees experience?), and as the weeks rolled by I kept thinking of the stage we would have been at if all had gone 'normally'; the date he was due, when he would have sat up and smiled, when he would have begun crawling. Mothers' Day that year was a hurdle as it was the date we had tentatively earmarked for his Thanksgiving service. Ever since then, we have been acutely aware of what a minefield Mothering Sunday can be for many people, for an infinite variety of reasons.

There was the difference in our personalities as well. Chris was used to hiding his emotions, as so many people do; the only time I have ever seen him cry was at Sarah's birth, although as the years have passed I have become more able to read his face and sense what is going on. I am much more open, and volatile, and find it difficult to put on any kind of front. He clearly felt that he had to be strong for me, not realizing that I needed him to show his pain as a sign that he was grieving too, and hadn't simply put it out of his mind. He took refuge in his work, keeping busy, and being determined to keep the show on the road. But ministry is relentless and never-ending; with eight chapels to look after, he was always tired and running to catch up with himself, and he began to question whether he could carry on. He wanted to do more to support me, but there weren't enough hours in the day, or days in the week. This didn't seem right to me; I felt that I should be able to manage without leaning on him to the extent that he was offering, but I also resented the fact that proper days off seemed to be so few and far between. Finding the time and the space to step off the treadmill to discuss what was happening was exceedingly difficult; were it not for our appointments with Hilary, I really wonder if we would have come through this together. In actual fact, we only needed three or four sessions; simply putting the time aside to meet together, to talk about our feelings, our hopes and fears for the future, and with a trusted third party to help us communicate, made all the difference, and cracks in that brick wall between us quickly appeared.

It is easy to see how couples might break up after losing a child, if they are not able to accept the differences between them. Grief places a tremendous strain on a partnership, not just because of the overwhelming sadness, but the other exhaustingly heavy baggage that goes with it; the sense of losing control is very threatening. We prided ourselves on being efficient when it came to day-to-day organization, and were quite nonplussed to discover that Chris had completely forgotten to attend a meeting of clergy one day in January, in Darlington. We would not even have been aware of it, had the secretary not written afterwards to assure us of the prayers and support of the other ministers, and to find out how we were. He had not expected Chris to attend, but had been surprised not to receive an apology. We wondered what other things had fallen by the wayside, or whom we might have inadvertently offended. There was a sense that our world might be unravelling around us, and we were powerless to stop it, which did nothing for our self-confidence or self-esteem. When only one partner is affected in this way, the other one can, hopefully, do something to assist; but when both are going downhill fast, there is a problem.

Before we were married, the minister who was preparing us told us it was the commitment that mattered, not our feelings. Love, he said, is an unreliable basis for a lasting relationship as sometimes it can disappear altogether. But if you hang on, knowing that you have promised to love each other, it will return, even grow. There were times when we could so easily have turned our backs on each other and walked away because the pain was too great and seemed insuperable:

> The cords of death encompassed me;
> the torrents of perdition
> assailed me;
> the cords of Sheol entangled me;
> the snares of death confronted me.
>
> (Psalm 18.4–5)

Sometimes I wonder what might have happened if Roy had not insisted on our having preparation sessions with him before the wedding; I remember more of what he said then than in the actual service.

It was shortly after that memorable episode in the kitchen, when we could so easily have fallen apart, that we received a letter from friends in Huntingdon, Ken and June Hebborn. Chris had known them since his days in the RAF, and they had always supported him through prayer after he left the air force and entered the ministry. When we were married, the prayers continued. They had rung us up a few times recently, and were clearly astute enough to realize that we were toiling more than we were letting on to anyone. How did they know the desperate straits we were in? As in my letters to Chris in the period shortly before he returned to Sierra Leone, when I was utterly miserable, it was more what was not said, than what we actually articulated, that gave the game away. At the end of February we were stunned to receive a cheque for £500 from their prayer group, with instructions that we should have a holiday, go away and get well.

I was in tears, as hope began to appear; Chris could no longer resist the prospect of a holiday, and just talking about possibilities lightened our spirits.

The following week he went into Cook's in Darlington and came back triumphantly having found a ten-day half-board offer at a hotel in Majorca. The next day another cheque arrived, from a member of the prayer group who had not been present on the day when they had decided what they were going to do; this one was for £50, for ice creams for Sarah. In the event we decided that would be too many for one little girl, so we had some too!

There were definite streaks of light beginning to appear now on the horizon. We have never been great ones for 'getting ready to go on holiday'; we simply didn't have the money for great shopping expeditions. But I enjoyed making two little dresses for Sarah, and tracking down a sunhat that fitted, as she had grown out of the one she had worn the previous summer. Kind friends volunteered to have Mop, and our neighbours offered to look after the cats and keep the boiler going – at that time of year we did not dare to let it go out! Before dawn on a snowy morning at the beginning of April, we drove up to Newcastle airport, and took off exactly on time. The consultant at the hospital had been very sceptical about allowing Sarah to fly because of the problems with her ears, but our GP overruled him and prescribed a nasal spray that we administered just before take-off, and in the event we had no problems at all. She ate about half a pound of grapes on the journey out, and about the same amount of strawberries coming home, and her ears clearly did not trouble her once.

The hotel was very comfortable, apart from the cot, which looked potentially lethal, so Sarah slept with us; the food was an excellent buffet, which suited us perfectly, although we nearly missed our dinner on the first night because we had omitted to put our watches forward an hour! The weather was kind, and we soaked up the sunshine as we played on the beach and explored the island. It was not yet high season; Majorca was stunningly beautiful with the spring blossom at its best, and the holiday did exactly what it had been intended to do. We came home feeling refreshed, healthy, and ready to face the future. The icing on the cake was that Sarah's ears had improved to the extent that the grommets were not required – the consultant was surprised, but we simply put it down to the power of prayer.

That holiday was a real turning point; Sarah's improving health and the fact that a hot summer followed were not insignificant factors. It did not mean that we had stopped grieving; far from it.

> I thought that I
> had passed
> from the storm
> into the calm,
> and that I

> could safely walk
> into the future
> without you
> the leviathan of grief
> catching me unawares,
> but I was
> wrong,
> for today
> you came again
> gripping me by the throat
> and shaking me like a dog
> with a hare.

Black days continued to arrive without any warning, but the spaces between them got longer. We did not necessarily go down together, and it became more possible to say to each other 'Help!' and for the other one to be able to offer the support that was needed. A sign that we were beginning to take hold of the initiative came when Chris announced one day that he was going to burn his old sermons. My heart was in my mouth; I love a good bonfire, but the sermon drawer in his filing cabinet had been a lifeline for us on the Saturdays when we faced Sunday without having found the time for the necessary sermon preparation. As it turned out, the removal of the crutch had the desired effect; he knew he had to make the time, and he did. He felt a lot better as a result, and because he felt better, I felt less threatened.

The next real hurdle came at the end of the year, when we started to try again for another baby. I now have the faintest glimmer of understanding of what couples must go through who have difficulties in conceiving; in fact it only took us a few months, but every month that passed seemed like a threat – what if we couldn't do it? This was the first time we had felt ourselves under any pressure to conceive, and it did absolutely nothing for our relationship; frankly, given the tension we were under, I am amazed that I conceived as quickly as I did. I had a nasty attack of bronchitis in the middle of this phase, which necessitated a course of antibiotics, and our GP advised us to put our plans on hold until I had completely recovered, which I found very frustrating. By March 1990, when my pregnancy was confirmed, we had come to appreciate that this was another thing no one should take for granted. Over the months I had become familiar with the Psalms, and had found some that really did not speak helpfully to our situation, e.g. Psalm 127.3: 'Sons are indeed a heritage from the Lord, the fruit of the womb a reward.' Fortunately, there were others to balance the picture, like Psalm 126.6: 'Those who go out weeping, bearing the seed for sowing, shall come home with shouts of joy, carrying their sheaves.' Together, we had to hope and trust in God.

6

Ben's Legacy

How many of us have dreams of the kind of person they would really like to have been, and the lifestyle they would have chosen had they been completely free to do so? Before we embarked on having a family, I had a vague picture in my mind of being a relaxed, untroubled mother with a whole brood of children, living in the country; we might not have a lot of money, but we would have sufficient to get by; the children would be well-spaced so that the older ones would look after their younger siblings. Because of the hurly-burly of family life, none of them would exhibit prima-donna tendencies, but would have the corners rubbed off from the start, and all would grow up to be happy, well-adjusted members of society. But life isn't like that, and children certainly don't develop according to any parent's plan, or even their own; I hasten to add that I always knew this was never going to happen! But in addition, I quickly realized that I was not especially gifted or happy when it comes to bringing up young children, and the process of childbearing was not easy for me. It is more than likely that the experience of Ben had a much more profound impact on me than I realized at the time.

'Relaxed, untroubled and care-free' is a description that had no relevance whatsoever to the way I felt about being a parent, however much I might have wished it otherwise. It is, of course, difficult to imagine how I would have felt had Ben not been born with his particular condition; his birth coincided with the stage in Sarah's life when she was just getting up on her feet and taking off, and we were all on uncharted territory. First-time parents are, we are told, prone to being more anxious anyway. I have a strong suspicion, however, that both Chris and I became more protective, and quite probably overprotective, as a result of losing Ben. My heart was in my mouth every time our toddler approached the top of the staircase in our manse in Hawes; I knew that she had to learn to come down the stairs on her own some day, but I hated the process of teaching her how to do it. I will never forget the relief I felt when, for the first time, I watched her turn around and lie on her tummy, feet pointing down the stairs, and then carefully crawling and sliding down on her own.

One day we were playing in the park in Hawes; Sarah had climbed to the top of the steps of the tall, old-fashioned slide, which was well over 12 feet high. Just as she got to the platform, some RAF planes chose to do a low overhead flying exercise, and roared above us, making an absolutely deafening racket. Sarah let go of the rails and clapped her hands over her ears – and wobbled. I nearly had heart failure; being pregnant at the time I could not move fast enough to rescue her, but fortunately a young friend who was with me leapt into the breach and raced up the ladder to hold her. I shook for hours afterwards (subsequently, I made it my mission to mount a campaign for a safe playground, the slide was eventually taken down, and new equipment and safety surfaces installed).

Another time, when playing on the beach, we took our eyes off her for what could only have been a matter of seconds; when we looked for her, all we could see was her sunhat on the water. Chris dashed into the sea and hauled her out, none the worse for her ducking. These were absolutely normal occurrences in the life of an active and inquisitive toddler, but I certainly did not take them in my stride! I was very conscious that, compared with many of my more relaxed friends, I was constantly on the go, supervising her every move. That was one reason why we wanted to have more than one child; I felt it would take the pressure off her somewhat – but it would be the same story with Nathan. It's like parental love; there seems to be enough anxiety to go round, regardless of the number of children you have!

The fact that my third pregnancy turned out to be a very anxious time is hardly to be wondered at. The staff at the Friarage Hospital in Northallerton were very reassuring from the start. As far as they were concerned, this was an absolutely normal pregnancy, and nothing special had to be organized. I was offered amniocentesis, but when I declined, that was accepted without question. No other tests were suggested. Today, it is very likely that Ben's condition might have been picked up long before he was born because of the more detailed scans and other tests which are now the norm, and we would have been offered a termination. We are thankful that this did not happen; at least we had a clean, straightforward grief with none of the 'what ifs' which many people have to contend with now. So we were not keen to have any extra tests during this pregnancy; they would just have complicated matters.

Everything went quite smoothly at first; it was wonderful to have my pregnancy confirmed in March, and I took comfort from my friends telling me that the more sick I was, the better chance I had of a happy outcome – an old wives' tale, no doubt, but reassuring nevertheless, as I was suffering from morning, noon and night sickness again.

We went on holiday in our caravan to the Yorkshire coast in the middle of June, while my mother and her cousin came to stay in the manse, and to look after Mop. Just three days into the holiday, my mother fell while walking the dog, and broke her hip. So she was carted off to Northallerton in an ambulance, and we came home – and Mop disappeared in her panic at being the cause of the fall! While Chris went off to the hospital, I raced up the road to try and track her down, and eventually found her in her favourite field where she had taken refuge. The next day we went to the Lake District for a few hours, determined we would salvage something of the holiday, and I began to lose blood. This was the first of a string of threatened miscarriages; the next was a couple of weeks later, after I had spent the afternoon at the town carnival.

I was put under strict orders to take things easy, and given another scan at the hospital to check that everything was in order. The scan was reassuring, and I then had to come to terms with leading a more restricted life than I was used to. This proved to be a challenge; how can one take it easy with an active toddler underfoot, unless someone comes and takes over? Our neighbours and friends were very supportive, and regularly took Sarah off for hours at a time, but I felt woefully inadequate, and uneasy at the amount of time she was being farmed out. The fact that she seemed blissfully happy playing with her friends next door made it just about tolerable, but I was not comfortable about it! I was probably far too sensitive about our dependence on our friends; people who lived near their extended families surrounded us, and received regular help with childcare as a matter of course. We were on our own. But it is always easier to give than to receive, and my problem was that I felt I was on the receiving end all the time.

The baby was due in the middle of November. After the August Bank Holiday, when I had spent much of the day encouraging Chris as he laid a new carpet in our caravan, I found myself in hospital, with contractions coming rather frequently. I was given an injection of surfactant to help the baby's lungs mature, and then we waited to see what materialized. Mercifully, nothing did; the contractions faded away, and after three days in hospital, I was allowed to go home, with strict instructions to do nothing. The midwife turned up and deposited a couple of large bags in our living room, containing everything that we would need for a home delivery, and the waiting game began. The cylinders of gas and air were a kind of comfort, sitting behind the door, but I knew I didn't want to have the baby at home if it could possibly be avoided. Memories of Ben's precipitate arrival were vivid; how would we have coped if it had happened at home?

This is interesting, because in theory I was, and still am, quite passionate about the way our western culture has sanitized birth and death, making it very clinical, and removing it from the normal rhythm of life. When I worked in Papua New Guinea I had a short stay in the local hospital and was struck by the way families cared for their own members, sleeping under the bed, providing food and care, and being intimately involved with the whole hospital process. There were no intensive care facilities available there of the type that hit me between the eyes when I flew home after my father had his stroke, to discover him being kept alive by various interventions which he hated. I know which kind of care we would all have opted for had we been given the choice at that time. Maybe we would have found it easier, in the long run, to live with the fact of Ben's death had he been born at home – I just don't know. But I recognized that I was very scared at the thought of possibly giving birth to our third child at home, 40 miles from the hospital, without the medical support that we might need.

So I settled into a quiet routine of moving from the sofa to the kitchen table, and back again, for the duration, which should have been another 12 weeks. Fortunately, I loved *Sesame Street*, which in those days was on television for an hour every day; I became an expert also in *Postman Pat* and *Fireman Sam*, and applied myself to sewing tapestry cushion covers whenever Sarah permitted. Our mothers took it in turns to come and stay, taking over the running of the household, and our neighbours, Gwen and Janet, simply adopted Sarah between them. I could not believe that this was really happening to me, was sure that somehow my symptoms had been brought on by anxiety, and that I could rise above it all. So one day towards the end of September, when Chris was taking his mother to the station at Darlington to swap her for my mother, who was travelling down from Edinburgh, I got off the sofa and proceeded to hang out the washing. The sun was shining, there was a light breeze, and I hated the thought of missing a good drying day!

By the time Chris came home, I knew I was in trouble. The doctor came, the ambulance was summoned, and I was whisked off to hospital again; 40 miles in the back of an ambulance, bumping along winding Dales roads when in labour, is an experience I would rather forget. I tried to insist that I could go either in the front of the ambulance, or in the car, but the paramedics would not have it. Chris followed in the car. Fortunately, the doctor managed to stop the labour once I was admitted, but this time I was not allowed to go home. I was told that I had to stay in bed and rest; again, I had some difficulty in believing that this was really serious, and got caught out by a midwife who found me downstairs one day. I simply could not seem to take on board that bedrest meant exactly that, apart from trips to the bathroom. After a week, my consultant came to see me, and said that he wanted to induce labour a couple of days later; he had a hunch that this baby would be better off out than in.

The next day I went into labour on my own accord. I had not even realized what was happening, but a routine test showed that the baby was on the way. A midwife went off to phone Chris, who was just about to go and take an assembly at the high school in Leyburn. He had my mother and Sarah in the car, as they had planned to continue their trip down the dale and visit me anyway. Chris was retrieved from the school hall by the secretary who had taken the message, and arrived post-haste; Sarah and Granny were parked in a dayroom next to the labour ward, and the fun began.

We had arranged that Hilary should deliver the baby if at all possible; she was on a day off, but was fortunately not very far away. I can recommend having a midwife who is also a good friend; the next two hours were almost fun – there was certainly a lot of laughter, which in the case of Chris and Hilary was not caused by gas and air. By this time we had made many friends in the maternity unit, and several interested health professionals dropped in to see how things were progressing and to encourage us. Nathan arrived in nice time for lunch, weighing in at over seven pounds, which made me profoundly thankful that he was six weeks early. After we had held him, he was whisked away for thorough checks, which he passed with flying colours.

He seemed to be absolutely fine. In the light of his prematurity, Hilary put a little hat on him, which he lost no time in pulling off and throwing on the floor. She tried two or three more times, but each offering was disdained, and eventually she had to give up the attempt. Sarah and my mother came to see him when he was only minutes old, then my mother looked after him while Chris and Sarah raced into town to buy some nappies and a teddy bear. I had steadfastly refused to get anything ready this time, as a kind of insurance against anything going wrong. Fortunately, the maternity unit had plenty of spare baby clothes we could borrow. Over the next few weeks Sarah would become expert at choosing his outfit for the day from the wardrobe in the Special Care Baby Unit.

I felt very well, and would have gone home more or less immediately were it not for the fact that the chapel in Hawes was hosting a youth weekend, and our house was going to be full of visitors. So we decided that discretion was the better part of valour, and arranged to stay in hospital for a few days, to get some peace. This was providential because when Nathan was three days old, he began to droop; he became floppy, and was no longer interested in feeding, and after a few hours I went to find a nurse to share my concern. Her initial reaction was quite dismissive, which did not altogether surprise me, as I was conscious that I could well be perceived as an overanxious mother. But by late in the evening, I was sure there was something wrong, and asked for help again.

This time the response was quite different; Nathan was carefully examined, and within minutes he had been taken to the Special Care Baby Unit. I was sent to wait in a small dayroom, and given the phone, while various tests, including a lumbar puncture, were carried out. The fear of meningitis loomed large. Picking up the phone to ring Chris was very hard; when he had left us that afternoon, there had been little indication of any problems, and now I really didn't know what to say, other than the bald facts. I didn't dare articulate my fears, but of course we both dreaded the worst-case scenario; all we could do was call on our friends to pray, and wait. If I had known the book of Psalms well enough, these words would have echoed what I was feeling as I sat and waited:

I commune with my heart in the night;
I meditate and search my spirit:
'Will the Lord spurn for ever,
and never again be favourable?
Has his steadfast love ceased for ever?
Are his promises at an end for all time?
Has God forgotten to be gracious?
Has he in anger shut up his compassion?'

(Psalm 77.6–9)

If Nathan were to die, I thought, that would be the end of any belief or trust I had in God. I can't compete with Job!

The next day was a Sunday. Chris took a couple of services and then came straight down to the hospital (looking back, we marvel at how he managed to do that, but we didn't know then exactly how ill Nathan was). The services had been in his diary for a long time, because it was a special weekend of celebration for the church in Darlington where he had been invited to preach, and he did not want to let them down. I had an emergency number to ring if necessary. My sister drove up from Sheffield, so I had company for the day, before Chris arrived late in the afternoon, and the vigil continued.

The paediatricians shared their anxieties and bafflement with us – no one seemed to know what was wrong, or could venture any opinion as to what was likely to happen, although no more symptoms had appeared, which was a good sign in itself. They could give us no reassurance, other than saying they thought they could keep Nathan where he was, and he would not have to be transferred to St James's, in Leeds. We had to wait for more results of the various tests and see what developed. Nathan was in an incubator, with a drip attached to his head administering antibiotics (the staff called it a Domestos cocktail, as they were giving a variety of drugs in the hope that something would work until they got the test results back from the laboratory), and a nasal gastric tube through which he was given my expressed milk. At least I could feed him, if indirectly – apart from that we felt utterly helpless.

So did the staff on the maternity unit; one of them commented that if anything were to happen to Nathan, they would not be able to offer the kind of support we had had after Ben's birth, because they were now too involved themselves. That was a kind of comfort, but in a very strange way. The maternity wing was quite small, and I had been there for a long time, and had made friends among the staff. One of the advantages of going to Hilary had been that we did not know her at all, and she could be trusted to be quite objective when she talked to us; should we, heaven forbid, need that kind of help again, it would be harder to find. The other side of the coin was the sense of being surrounded by people who were genuinely concerned, and this made the experience less stressful than it might otherwise have been – we felt at home on the unit.

Nathan was ill for a week; he did not deteriorate, but he did not get better in a hurry either. We were encouraged by visits and messages from many friends, some of whom clearly found it very difficult when they saw him. On one occasion, a senior minister was visiting, and Sarah asked him if he would like to be taken to see her baby brother. She took him by the hand and led him into Nathan's little room; the poor man took one look and nearly fainted, clearly disconcerted by seeing all the tubes and wires. Fortunately Chris saw what was happening and pushed him into a chair before disaster struck. We laughed – after our friend had gone! There was a classic occasion when my sister offered to collect the baby's urine sample; she stood by the incubator for hours, holding the equipment and getting cramp in her hand; the moment she looked away, Nathan performed, and she missed it. Moments of humour kept us going, along with signs of hope, such as the fact that through it all Nathan tolerated his feeds wonderfully well.

Eventually he turned the corner, and we were told that he was going to be fine. His temperature stabilized, he became more alert, the medication was gradually reduced, and I began to feed him myself. We never did find out what had been wrong; he had picked up some kind of infection, possibly *in utero*, but it ran its course, and Nathan made a full recovery. We took ourselves off to our favourite café in Northallerton and treated ourselves to apple strudel to celebrate. At this point, a pleasant chapter began in my life; there was a very nice, private suite adjacent to the Special Care Unit, with a double bed, complete with candlewick bedspread, and en suite facilities. I was moved into this luxurious accommodation, and was eventually joined by my son, when he was allowed to leave Special Care. At first he was monitored very closely, but slowly the supervision was relaxed, until eventually we were leading as near to a normal life as one can lead in hospital. I had a happy time pushing him between my suite and the Special Care Unit in his goldfish bowl of a cot, to which a helium balloon had been attached – whenever anyone wanted to know where we were, they looked for the balloon.

It was a real treat to have a few happy, relaxed days; we were finally sent home when Nathan was two weeks old, by which time I felt fit and ready for anything. The final piece of equipment to go was his apnoea monitor, which indicated when there were any irregularities in his breathing. I did not realize until we no longer had it just how much I had come to rely on it; for a long time afterwards, I was terrified of going over to his cot and finding he had stopped breathing, and therefore never relaxed when he was asleep. What an irony – it is normal to rejoice when one's baby has finally dropped off to sleep, and to seize the opportunity to catch up with odd jobs, or one's own sleep, but it would not work out like that for me because of my fears. I have learned recently that 80 per cent of mothers who have some kind of 'neonatal need' (worries about a child at birth, and experience of Special Care treatment), suffer from a degree of depression afterwards. I can understand why.

It was as well that I had had that halcyon interlude; the evening we arrived home, Chris was catapulted into crisis mode with the news that his colleague in Leyburn was quite seriously ill. He was left dealing with 17 chapels on his own, and it was many months before the situation became manageable, and a lay worker was employed. Prior to this we had reached the decision that we would not have any more children, recognizing that we had had all the stress we thought we could handle. I was adamant that I could not face another pregnancy, whatever the circumstances, but did not want to deprive Chris of the opportunity for having more children, should that ever be a possibility. So I went into hospital for surgery a few weeks later, taking Nathan with me – he had the time of his life, and was only brought to me to be fed, spending the rest of the time at the nurses' station, being royally entertained. So much for my dreams of a brood of half a dozen children!

The name Nathan means 'gift of God'. On the day he was born, our friend Clare was walking on the hills with her husband, and took a wonderful photograph of a rainbow over the dales, which we have treasured ever since; it picked up George Matheson's words:

I trace the rainbow through the rain,
And feel the promise is not vain,
That morn shall tearless be.

(*Hymns & Psalms* 685)

We had sung that hymn at Ben's funeral.

We had our Service of Thanksgiving at the end of December, when Nathan was nearly four months old, and friends came from far and near, battling with some rather dubious weather conditions to be with us. Clare's husband, Boris, officiated, as he had at Sarah's service three years before. Chris was frantically busy in the circuit, but we were both agreed that we had to find ways of expressing our gratitude for Nathan's life, and all that had happened. The phrase 'There but for the grace of God' echoed in my head. According to the *Concise Oxford Dictionary of Quotations*, it is attributed to John Bradford, a Protestant martyr under Mary Tudor, who had engaged in a debate on predestination versus free will when he was in prison prior to his execution; he is reported to have said this when he saw some criminals being taken for execution. Although I could not embrace his theology, it served to remind me that many other people experience suffering and tragedy, and have to live with it on a day-to-day basis, which seems to have no end. We knew that if Ben had lived, our lives would have taken a radically different direction as we did our utmost to care for him, with all his needs. Now we had a healthy young family; how were we going to hold in tension the memories of what had gone before, alongside our joy for what we now had? We were clear that we must not take the gift of our children for granted. We had learned, from the reading we had done in the past couple of years, that approximately one in four of all pregnancies end in miscarriage (remember that this figure includes pregnancies that may never have been diagnosed), and a significant proportion of all couples fail to have their families exactly as they would have planned them, with no hitches of any kind along the way. That would indicate a great need for support of various kinds; what could we offer?

The answer came through my decision to train as a breastfeeding counsellor with the National Childbirth Trust. I had not found breastfeeding an easy thing to do at first, particularly when Sarah was tiny; when Nathan had to be fed through a nasal-gastric tube, I had to use an electric pump to express milk for him, and that brought its own problems. It was not something that felt natural, and when I was anxious and tense, the milk did not flow. I had a real sense of achievement when I managed to produce more than a teaspoonful of milk, and eventually settled into a routine of sessions with the pump that worked. Sitting beside Nathan and watching him as he lay in his incubator was helpful. He seemed so tiny and vulnerable, lying curled up in the foetal position, occasionally crying very faintly, like a kitten. At least this was something positive and constructive I could do for him. In the week of convalescence we spent together attached to the Special Care Baby Unit, I did my best to help other mothers who were struggling with the pump experience; the staff were rushed off their feet and very grateful that I had the time to help. I knew that the NCT offered training, and talked it over with the midwives, who were very keen that I should explore the possibility. The idea was that I would then be able to come back and offer what time I could to the unit; I envisaged it as being perhaps a weekly exercise, given the distance that we lived from the hospital.

When I began to make enquiries, we discovered that the only way I would be able to do the training was as a semi-distance learning student, going to Carlisle once every six weeks or so for an all-day tutorial on a Saturday with other trainees. Some training weekends at the NCT headquarters in London were also required, and the training would take two years, if I worked hard at it. I could not have contemplated pursuing the idea if Chris had not completely supported me in it; he was very happy to come with me to Carlisle, and take Sarah off for the day, while Nathan and I got on with the course; once he became mobile, he joined the family on their expeditions, and left me to my studies. We had some adventures; Carlisle was 70 miles away and sometimes the weather was not conducive to travel. We set off one day in torrential rain; coming home at dusk, when we were only about two miles from home, we found the water lapping over the top of the stone dyke at the side of the road, and the road itself was flooded. I got out of the car, only to find the water was at the top of my wellingtons; we were pondering what to do when we met our doctor coming the other way in his Range Rover. He told us to follow him, and his car made a bow-wave which cleared the way for us to get on to another road which took us over the hills and down into Hawes by another route.

When it came to the weekends I had to spend in London, family and friends came to the rescue. I could stay with my aunt, who was very pleased to see me; friends stayed with Chris and the children, and made Sundays possible. Ironically, it was my last weekend away that completed the weaning process, but by then Nathan was 18 months old, and I had decided it was high time the deed was done!

I gained a tremendous amount from the training, not least in listening and adult education skills; it was exactly the right thing for me to be doing at that time. As part of basic counselling training, I had to talk about my experience of parenting so far, and was thoroughly debriefed, which was really helpful.

I never did get to work back at the Friarage Hospital; we moved to Norfolk in the summer of 1993, just after I had qualified, so my training was put to use in a completely different geographical area. It was a shock to find that the NCT was not particularly welcome at the local hospital, but there was a very active group in the region, and plenty of opportunities to offer support to people who were looking for it. This became my work for the next six years; I taught antenatal classes, took my turn at the weekly drop-in session in a local health centre, and visited people in their homes (or had them in mine) when there were difficulties that I could help with. It was hugely rewarding; to come away from homes knowing that my visit had made a difference, and that mothers now had the confidence to keep on feeding their babies, and the fathers, or other family members, were reassured, was immensely worthwhile.

In time, I went on to do more training, so that I could become a tutor to trainees, which gave me more adult education experience, so that when the time eventually came to call it a day, I had transferable skills which made my return to the world of theological education quite straightforward. Around the time that I was offered a job in ministerial training, there was also a possibility of some paid employment for me with the local health authority. I had to weigh up my options carefully; in the end I decided that there were probably a few people around who might be interested in the health care job, but that there were not so many with my particular and peculiar qualifications for the academic one. But I had a strong sense that God's hand had been on me throughout, that my time working with new parents had been very rich, and had given me a purpose and identity in life outside the Church that I had badly needed. Nothing is wasted; what I experienced in those years had moulded me, and given me insights and understandings that stand me in good stead for what I do today.

Ben influenced our lives in many profound ways. As a family, we needed to find a means of remembering him, which did not feel contrived, or as if we were over-egging the pudding. Thanks to the foresight and care of the hospital staff, we had a photograph, but did not feel this was the kind of thing we wanted to display on the mantelpiece; I was very touched to discover some years later that my mother kept hers in her prayer book, and clearly treasured it. I compiled an album, which contained the photo, and the photograph from the one scan I had had, which was very fuzzy. We added his birth and death certificates, the letter we had received from the consultant afterwards, and various cards from friends that had been especially helpful. Kingsley Barrett's sermon notes went in, and other bits and pieces which referred to Ben in some way, or reminded us of him, such as St John Chrysostom's writing about the loss of a child:

> ... the deceased has moved into a better country, and bounded away to a happier inheritance; ... thou hast not lost thy son, but bestowed him henceforward in an inviolable spot. Say not then, I pray thee, I am no longer called 'father', for why art thou no longer called so, when thy son abideth? For surely thou didst not part with thy child, nor lose thy son?

Rather, thou hast gotten him, and hast him in greater safety. Wherefore, no longer shalt thou be called 'father' here only, but also in heaven; so that thou hast not lost the title 'father', but hast gained it in a nobler sense; for henceforth thou shalt be called father not of a mortal child, but of an immortal ... For think not, because he is not present, that therefore he is lost; for had he been absent in a foreign land, the title of thy relationship had not gone from thee with his body.

(John Chrysostom,
from Homily I on II Corinthians,
quoted in *All in the End is Harvest*, p. 52)

One of the cards was of two field mice climbing up a stalk of wheat, with the text 'except a grain of wheat fall into the ground' (John 12.24). Chris had begun to develop a hobby of doing cross-stitch; both Sarah and Nathan were given cross-stitch pictures by friends to welcome them into the world, so Chris did one for Ben based on the picture, and it hangs with the others in our living room. Next to it is a photograph of the place in Dentdale where we scattered his ashes. Whenever we are in the vicinity we try to go there; it is a lovely spot, in a small valley with a brook running through it, and is one of those special family places that means a lot to each of us in our different ways. We have had some great picnics there.

Christmas is of course a time for remembering his birthday as well, and I am sure that the way the festival is tinged with sadness has helped us to value it for what it really is. Making our gingerbread house on his birthday is as much a part of Christmas as anything else for us. Even if we do not quite manage to do it on the actual date, because of carol services or other work commitments, we make sure we put it in our diaries for somewhere around 17 December. In fact, the one we made the year he was born was actually produced the week before he arrived. We have a photograph of that occasion, with me helping Sarah to do the decorating – it is *just* apparent that I was pregnant, while most other photos of that time do not reveal Ben's presence at all.

There is almost a ritual element about how we go about it now; the family gathers around a sweet stall in the market, and everyone chooses what they want to put on the house; we then proceed to bake the gingerbread (which comes out differently every year, and sometimes causes enormous problems when the construction begins). Chris is the chief architect, and sets to with knives and cocktail sticks to build the house; meanwhile I make the icing, with which the family then proceeds to cover the house. The fun really begins at that point, when the sweets are attached; we all have our own style for edging the windows, doing the roof tiles, etc., and it is as well that the house has four walls, so we can each do our own thing on our particular section. Left-over icing goes to make the garden, with scraps of gingerbread forming bushes, and jelly babies cavort with snowmen.

Every year I try to argue my case for putting a little night-light inside the house, as we did when I was small; most years I fail, because we have not managed to make a proper window out of which the light could shine, as the gingerbread is too brittle, but I live in hope! Chris objects to the smell of singed gingerbread, which is another obstacle – but one day I will get my way. Then the house is displayed on the piano, and stays there, getting steadily harder, for the week or so of festivities. Normally it gets broken up and consumed around New Year, by which time it is rock hard and a danger to fragile teeth, but that does not put many children off!

When we still lived in Hawes, and before the children's activities added a real element of chaos to the period before Christmas, we would go to a family friendly fish and chip restaurant in Skipton, for Ben's 'birthday treat'; everyone else in the family has a treat, so we wanted to do the same for him. When we moved to Norfolk, that fell by the wayside, but it no longer mattered; Ben's place in our memories was assured. In choosing how we wanted to remember him, and adopting certain traditions, we were able to take some control of how and what we remembered, which made it manageable for us.

A good friend took up woodwork as a hobby, and the year after Ben was born produced a couple of lovely red tree ornaments, a heart and a star. One was for Sarah, and one was in memory of Ben. Two years later she arrived with a third, a moon, which belongs to Nathan. Little things like this have meant a great deal to me, and the ability of some people to think themselves into our situation, and be imaginative and creative in their response, has meant a great deal. Our children are very sensitive; when it comes to decorating the tree they always bring me Ben's star and stay close by as I put it on the tree. This is a special moment for reflection when I give thanks for Ben and all that he has meant to me and to the family, and pray for others who may be going through a similar trauma. It is very poignant; Ben completely changed the lenses through which I view life in general.

7

A Journey of Faith

I have read many books and articles by people who have wonderful stories to tell about how their faith helped them through particular crises or turning points in their lives. They are inspirational. In my case, however, the story was turned on its head; very often I felt as if my faith was being challenged and questioned, and at times it all but disappeared. This had a sequel 14 years after Ben's death, when we had to confront two more bereavements in quick succession. There is no triumphant conclusion; the journey continues, and my own spirituality and faith are never static. Questions, questions and more questions were what I found myself grappling with; the process has not ended yet. Sometimes I wonder if I would ever have moved into this searching mode, were it not for the pain of bereavement; who can tell? The pace of everyday life is such that unless a crisis hits, there is little incentive to look beyond what one has always taken for granted. Losing Ben stopped me in my tracks; my religion most certainly was not a comfort blanket to help me through the unbearable days, but eventually I came to understand that God was there, sharing the pain with us.

I was born into a Christian family and took God utterly for granted, as an integral part of my life. When the going was tough, as of course it was on occasion throughout my childhood and teenage years, it never occurred to me to question his existence, or to doubt his interest in me and my concerns. My father was a minister and an academic theologian; the great majority of our family friends were Christian, and the friends I made at school were mostly regular in their church attendance and involved in the life of various congregations. I was reluctant to join a youth group, being very conscious of the 'minister's daughter' label, and most of my social life revolved around music. But whenever I could, I would go and hear one of the great preachers who were active at the time, such as William Barclay and James Stewart. They preached no watered down version of Christianity, but gave their listeners plenty to think about. Half-hour sermons are rare these days, but when a good preacher gets going, half an hour seems like ten minutes. Looking back, I think I bypassed the 'milk' stage of faith and theology, and moved on to the 'meat' quite quickly (1 Corinthians 3.2), in theory at least, if not in practice. My faith had not yet been put to the test.

I remember that my father tried to get us to join with him every day in family prayers, but once my elder brother and sister became teenagers, it was a forlorn hope. As clergy children, we had a profound suspicion of overt piety, and as a result developed very individual and private ways of nourishing our spiritual lives. It would not have occurred to me to go to sleep without reading the Bible and saying my prayers, but neither did it register with me that there might be other ways of getting to know God. That was a discovery I would make at university. But the evangelical tradition of a strict 'quiet time' never quite worked for me; I was suspicious of being too disciplined because it seemed to me that it could border on the concept of salvation by works, which the Lutheran part of my background abhorred. This is odd, as by nature I like structure and discipline. I realize now that there was a complex set of factors at work in me, and a strong influence was my determination to find my *own* way forward, and not to do as I was told or expected!

I could not imagine doing a job which did not have a strong vocational element to it. Ordination was not an option; I was aware that I carried too much baggage from being the daughter of a well-known minister. But teaching was another matter, and I developed a real passion for making Church history accessible to people who might have been put off the subject because of poor experiences of history teaching at school. After teaching for three years in a sixth form college, I was confronted with a decision: should I go for promotion, and buy a bigger house and a fridge-freezer (which somehow epitomized western materialism in my eyes), or should I be brave and see if my skills could be of use to the Church overseas? I was delighted to be offered a post at Rarongo Theological College in Papua New Guinea, which was how I came to meet Chris at the training college in Selly Oak, Birmingham, for Methodists going overseas. I was determined I would not marry a minister, but eventually recognized that I had met my match.

His background was quite different from mine, and when I went to meet his family for the first time I was literally quaking in my shoes, because his mother and brothers were members of the Church of Jesus Christ of Latter Day Saints (better known as 'Mormons'). Chris had had a conversion experience when he was working in Saudi Arabia, and shortly after that had left the air force to start training for the Methodist ministry. I thought I knew and understood Methodism, but I had never encountered the Mormons. When we went to meet each other's families, my father put Chris through a theological inquisition, which he passed with flying colours; Chris's mother was so relieved that her son had found a wife, there were no difficulties put in our way, and we resolved to avoid talking about faith or theology if it looked as if it would cause upset in either family!

During our two-year engagement, when we were apart, we wrote to each other every couple of days, trying to understand each other's viewpoints as well as we could. This was vital, as we were coming from such different places, and also living through very diverse experiences in our current posts. When my father had the stroke which led to his death, we were able to be together in Edinburgh for ten days, and did some more hard talking, thinking and praying. The upshot was the decision not to go to Sierra Leone together after our marriage, but to settle in the UK, to be as near as possible to my parents, which is how we came to be in Wensleydale – although my father had, in fact, died by the time we moved there. This was my first experience of real grief, but I did not recognize its impact at the time. My mother needed support in the first instance; then I had to find a temporary job, as it was decided by the church not to send me back to Papua New Guinea for only six months. My period of temporary employment was a miserable experience for me, in that I was teaching a subject that was unfamiliar (geography), in difficult circumstances, as I had picked up the timetable of a teacher who had left suddenly. I ended up close to having a nervous breakdown, and simply walked out one day – an action that took me literally years to accept and come to terms with. This was my first desert experience, in terms of spiritual isolation and desolation, although I was struggling too much to be able to recognize it for what it was. Chris picked it up from my letters; he commented that they were masterpieces of revealing nothing.

When we married, I was still in a very shaky position. Now I can see that this was because of a whole series of losses, coming in quick succession: loss of father, career, self-confidence, self-respect, independence and identity – all in the space of less than a year. There was hardly a part of my life that had not been affected in some way by loss; in my adult life I have never weighed as little as I did then! After the honeymoon we set about gathering up our belongings from where they were stored around the country, and moved to Hawes, straight into the pressures of a very busy rural circuit. I thought I knew what was involved in being a minister's wife, but discovered I had a great deal to work out. My mother had never been a minister's wife in any kind of context that remotely resembled where I found myself! I struggled with not having a job for the first time since I had left university, and realized how much emphasis our society places on paid employment. As a result, one of the things I have learned not to ask a stranger is 'What do you do?'

Rural Methodism was an eye-opener to me. Chris had responsibility for eight chapels; he was in his element, and apart from always having far too much to do and feeling he was never on top of things, he was on familiar territory. I found myself trying to attach names to scores of new faces, many of which belonged to elderly stalwarts of the church, and I worked hard to understand what was motivating each individual and chapel congregation. Village identity was everything, and the Methodist church often fulfilled a vital role in keeping that alive, but the congregations generally were small, the majority of members over 60, and represented a time and culture with which I was quite unfamiliar. In many ways the training I had received at Selly Oak, prior to going out to Papua New Guinea, was of more use to me in the Yorkshire Dales.

In Papua New Guinea, going to church was often a vibrant, colourful and exciting experience, particularly when the people taking the service had worked at contextualizing the worship, something which was just beginning to emerge when I was there; this was a period when people were exploring genuine Melanesian ways to worship, which were not simply western adaptations. It was very different in my new home circuit. I was in the habit of going to church and judging the worship by how 'good' I thought it was, and what I felt I had received from it; more often than not I came away quite empty. So the pattern developed that I was not unhappy if I could not go to church on a particular Sunday, perhaps because Sarah or I were unwell. I even noted in my diary on one occasion when we were on holiday, how much I appreciated staying at home and reading the Sunday papers! The idea that I might be drawn by my love of God to go to church simply to offer myself in worship was one which dawned on me only slowly, several years later.

When we were first married, we started out with every intention of reading the Bible and praying together regularly. But it didn't work out for various reasons. I got up and went to bed earlier than Chris; he would come in late most evenings after being at a meeting, and during the day his schedule was so unpredictable, we couldn't find a regular time. We kept an open house, so had a constant stream of visitors coming through the door, some of whom stayed for several days. The last straw was late one evening when we were praying in bed and Chris came out with 'God bless the lawnmower' before falling asleep.

After that, as a rule, we did our own thing with our devotions, although in times of crisis we would stop and pray, and that felt absolutely right and uncontrived for us both. Much later on, we started a regular Tuesday morning prayer time with some of the local church members, which was very successful – just having someone else coming in gave us a structure and a discipline we couldn't maintain ourselves. But that is another story.

It felt as if I was ploughing rather a lonely furrow in terms of my own spiritual life and understanding of what I was meant to be doing; I could find some sense of identity in being married to Chris and starting a family, but it was not enough. I had big questions about the Church, mission and ministry, and where I fitted in. I had foreseen some of these problems when we were first engaged; I was used to being an independent and articulate (and yes, sometimes troublesome) church member, and had decided that I would have to take a back seat once we were married, as I did not want to fall out with anyone, perhaps even with my husband, in public. I chose not to become involved in church politics for fear of making life awkward for Chris, so kept away from all the meetings that I would have gone to as a matter of course in the days before I married a minister. This was highly frustrating; after a church council or circuit meeting, I would be on tenterhooks until Chris got home and could tell me what had happened. It seemed so much harder to be involved in Britain than it had been overseas! Spiritual high points were to be savoured and remembered, to keep me going the rest of the time. Driving home from the hospital after Sarah's birth was one of those moments; my heart was full of love and thanksgiving to God for our daughter and for all the promises she brought with her. I could join with the psalmist in praise, and blessed the Lord with all my soul (Psalm 104). Gradually, through attendance at the health visitor's clinic, and similar venues, I began to make friends with the young families in the neighbourhood, and possibilities of a new direction in work with children and families emerged; this was something I could do in my own right.

Just when it seemed as if I was finding my feet, Ben arrived. I have often wondered why we did not feel guilty about what happened – it would have been so easy to think that this was perhaps a punishment from God because we had not planned the pregnancy, and had not greeted the news of it with delight. Yet I can honestly say that this was one emotion we did not experience, probably because neither of us could entertain for a moment the notion of a God who punishes, in the style that Job's comforters propounded. Of course we had feelings of regret; I wondered if I had let Ben down in some way, because I had not felt happy about the pregnancy. But several health professionals said to us on various occasions that it is remarkable how many mothers sense that something is wrong, which prevents their 'owning' the pregnancy in the normal way.

Some friends found it strange that our immediate response was not to question God. We never asked, 'Why has this happened to us?' or 'What kind of God would allow this to happen?' Those questions were simply not appropriate to our situation, or our faith. We both had friends who had had babies who had died shortly after birth, we knew that these things happened and that we were on much firmer ground if we were to ask, 'Why *not* us?' Job had had the same response: 'Shall we receive the good at the hand of God, and not receive the bad?' (Job 2.10).

In the same way, my understanding of God did not lead me, at least not immediately, to doubt his love or care for us; I did not hold him responsible in any way for what had happened. But quite what he was doing, and where he was, while we were struggling, was not clear. It was only several years later, after I started work again in theological education, that I began to grapple academically with the concept of the suffering God and realized that this was what we had instinctively believed at the time of Ben's death. God was weeping with us, as Jesus had wept at Lazarus' tomb in John 11.35 (Paul Fiddes, 'Suffering, divine', in *Modern Christian Thought*, pp. 633–6). 'The Lord is near to the broken-hearted' (Psalm 34.18) was initially more helpful than the words of the much loved Psalm 91, which speaks of God's deliverance from all sorts of terrors.

In the days after Ben died, the friends who came and simply sat with me, without saying anything, were the people I valued the most. But oddly, sensing that they represented God, who was sitting at the bottom of the pit with me, meant that I felt he was not a great deal of help. I was nothing if not irrational! I was having to grow up fast and move on from an understanding of a God who could solve my problems for me, to one who might not be able to do anything other than suffer next to me, and that the suffering was actually costly, because of its helplessness. I came back, time and again, to the conviction that God did not create us as puppets but gave us free will and freedom of choice; when he did that he relinquished the right to intervene and stop us getting it wrong. I might take this as a starting point:

> The Lord looks down from heaven;
> he sees all humankind.
> From where he sits enthroned he watches
> all the inhabitants of the earth –
> he who fashions the hearts of them all,
> and observes all their deeds.
>
> (Psalm 33.13–15)

But I had to move on in my understanding, because of what the incarnation means; this was total involvement with the human predicament, even if it was not a magic wand to put things right.

Where can I go from your spirit?
Or where can I flee from your presence?
If I ascend to heaven, you are there;
if I make my bed in Sheol, you are there.
If I take the wings of morning
and settle at the farthest limits of the sea,
even there your hand shall lead me,
and your right hand shall hold me fast.

(Psalm 139.7–10)

If the only thing God was doing was to hold me fast, that would have to do for now.

The disaster of Chernobyl had happened not that long before (April 1986); within a six-month period after Ben's birth there was an unusual cluster of birth defects and cot deaths in our vicinity, and we did wonder if there was any connection. Was not this a classic example of humanity doing its own thing, and getting it badly wrong? A research project eventually showed that this was not the case, and the cluster was 'just one of those things'. We were not desperate for answers, other than to find out if there was any reason why we could not try for another child in due course; once that was clarified, we could put this questioning to one side, recognizing that we were very fortunate. We had friends who had not been so lucky, because they carried genes that conspired against having a healthy child; we could only glimpse a shadow of what they must have experienced.

The fact remained, however, that I had given birth to a severely handicapped child. Psalm 139 was again a real comfort to me, although I know these verses have caused grief and even fury to many people who have faced similar circumstances to ours:

For it was you who formed my inward parts;
you knit me together in my mother's womb.
I praise you, for I am fearfully and wonderfully
made.
Wonderful are your works;
that I know very well.
My frame was not hidden from you,
when I was being made in secret,
intricately woven in the depths of the earth.
Your eyes beheld my unformed substance.
In your book were written
all the days that were formed for me,
when none of them as yet existed.

(Psalm 139.13–17)

For me the key phrase was, and still is, 'fearfully and wonderfully made'. This could be translated as 'I praise you, for I am awesomely wonderful' (Kidner, *Psalms 73–150*, p. 465). Chris took this as an illustration of the amazement he felt when he saw Ben and discovered the extent of his condition; for him, it was a minor miracle that he was born alive at all. For me, it was rather different. I held in tension the information we had been given, that something had gone wrong with the development of Ben from the earliest moments of conception, with a question about his place in creation. Was he imperfect in God's eyes? Is there not a great deal more to creation than we can hope to understand? This was Job's conclusion: 'Therefore I have uttered what I did not understand, things too wonderful for me, which I did not know' (Job 42.3), and it is the way Psalm 139.17 develops its thought: 'How weighty to me are your thoughts, O God!'

I recently watched a television programme about genetic mutations, and I was so annoyed I had to turn it off; the attitude of the presenter was voyeuristic, patronizing and ghoulish, taking no account of the individual people who had been involved in each case, and their stories. I had to affirm Ben's individuality, the fact that he was a person in his own right, with a story to tell. He was not sent to us as a punishment for our sins, or as a test to see how we performed; nor was he simply a tool to make us better people, in effect an educational aid. But:

> Who among all these does not know
> that the hand of the Lord has done this?
> In his hand is the life of every living thing
> and the breath of every human being.
>
> (Job 12.9–10)

Why should we have all the answers? The bottom line for me was my belief in the God of love, who loved Ben as much as he did the rest of 'perfect' humankind.

I was no Pollyanna, however, able to give thanks in all circumstances. For many weeks I felt utterly lost, and was groping my way through a fog with no landmarks visible. My Bible lay on my bedside table and remained closed, unless I turned to the Psalms, which I did from time to time, in a voyage of discovery; the writers of the psalms of lament echoed what I was feeling.

> I am weary with my moaning;
> every night I flood my bed with tears;
> I drench my couch with my weeping.
> My eyes waste away because of grief.
>
> (Psalm 6.6–7)

That in itself was a consolation; if people of faith could despair in that way, I was not unique; sometimes the psalmist shouted at God, and I could identify with that as well, when particular crises intervened.

Why, O Lord, do you stand so far off?
Why do you hide yourself in times of trouble?

(Psalm 10.1)

Most of the time, I felt as if I was not in contact. I
have observed this in my day-to-day relationships
with friends; when I am particularly stressed or
depressed, I go to ground, and cannot make the effort
to pick up the phone, and it was like that with God. I
wasn't in a place where I could speak to him, nor was
I in a mood to listen. There were two particular low
points, the first being the night Sarah became ill and
we had to race to the hospital; the second was after
Nathan's birth when he became very poorly and was
taken away to the Special Care Baby Unit for a
lumbar puncture and other tests. On both of those
occasions I can vividly remember asking God exactly
what he thought he was doing – and then abandoning
prayer, yet knowing (and taking comfort from the
fact) that friends were praying for us. A crutch?
Perhaps. But why not use one when it is needed? I
would have felt utterly bereft and exposed if I had not
been able to call on friends for that kind of support.
'In the shadow of your wings I will take refuge, until
the destroying storms pass by' (Psalm 57.1) – rational
theology had no influence over me at those points,
but blind, instinctive, faith remained.

The action of the prayer group in Huntingdon
when they sent us the cheque for a holiday marked a
breakthrough for me, not just in terms of cutting
through the cycle of despair that had taken hold, but
because of what it represented concerning the power
of prayer. These were people who had always
supported us in all that we did; now they were
literally putting their money where their mouths
were. Slowly I came to understand that this was a
superb example of the sacrifice and costliness of
prayer; it is no good simply rattling off names and

situations where we would like God to take the initiative and sort matters out. We have to be prepared to be his instruments in the process. Ever since then, when we have been in particular need, we have known we can call on that group, and they will engage in focused, fervent prayer that actually demands a great deal in terms of time and energy.

In February 1991, a few months after Nathan was born, it was my turn. Our friends Pauline and Dave Kendall rang to say that their third baby, Joshua, had been born, and was critically ill in Great Ormond Street Hospital with a liver problem. His older sister, Alex, had been born in the summer of 1986 and died a couple of weeks later because of a diseased liver; six weeks after Sarah was born, Luke had arrived, fully healthy; and now he had a little brother. That night I prayed as I had never prayed before. The fact that my favourite *Inspector Morse* programme was on television was irrelevant; I knelt and hammered at the gates of heaven (that is what it felt like!) and harangued God for several hours: 'The Lord hears when I call to him' (Psalm 4.3). At the end of it I was utterly exhausted, but knew that I had been heard. When Chris came home, I told him what had happened, and we continued to pray, along with hundreds of others around the country, for a couple of months, until Joshua was discharged from hospital. He continued to be under the care of Great Ormond Street for some years, but he made a steady recovery, and is now fully well – an unexplained miracle in the eyes of the doctors.

I would like to be able to say that my prayer life was transformed as a result of these experiences. In some important ways it was: I believed again in the power of prayer, and could engage with God again, but always with the proviso that he is not a problem-solver. It is a much more mysterious process and involves more than I can fathom, but it is a life-changing activity. We attended a conference for returned missionaries in the early summer of 1988, and met a delightful Roman Catholic priest who had recently returned from Latin America. He commented that he had long since abandoned any attempt to pray regularly, in a time and space set apart from the bustle of the world; he had to pray as he went along, snatching moments of communication as best he could. That struck a chord with us both; Chris, more than I, had been feeling guilty about his failure to find a regular time for prayer and Bible reading, and this view of things was helpful. That is not to say that we were opting out, or regarding prayer as less important than the pressing business of day-to-day living. But we could finally accept that our spiritual life was precious to us, even if it was somewhat undisciplined and erratic. When I emerged from the desert experience of the early months of 1989, I was able to pick up that style of prayer again – the great thing was that I was on speaking terms with God once more. I continue to work at finding new ways, and places to pray; these days the time I spend on trains, or walking, are very helpful. Driving is not ideal, as I tend to get so immersed I am in danger of being distracted!

Spiritually, I was finding my feet again. It felt as if it was time to become rather more proactive with regard to my Christian discipleship and what that meant in terms of ministry than I had been for some years. As the channel of communication with God opened up, I found myself preaching on various occasions. I didn't look for them, but they seemed to find me. I had never regarded preaching as something I particularly wanted to do, or felt called to. This stemmed from my upbringing – a great deal of emphasis had been placed on good and sound preaching, and I knew I could never measure up to the standards that had been set. I was somewhat put out when I discovered that I was expected to preach regularly in Papua New Guinea, but at least none of my family would be there to listen to me! I felt quite inadequate for the task, fully conscious that I had much more to learn from the people I was working and living with than I could teach them. But it was part of the job, and I did the best I could.

In Wensleydale, I spoke at a few services and meetings as part of what was expected of me as a returned missionary, but after a couple of years asked if I could stop, because the political situation in Melanesia was changing so rapidly I could no longer speak about it with any authority. However, even without the returned missionary label, I was asked to take various services, and felt that it was right to do so. Gradually I gained in confidence, helped by the way in which members of the congregation encouraged me afterwards, and began to ask why I was not a local preacher (the Methodist Church has always depended on, and valued, the work of lay people who are authorized to take services and preach).

Our group of churches was not blessed with an over-abundance of preachers, and often chapels were asked to make their own arrangements for services when no preacher was available. I felt I could offer them something, building on the urgent need I had felt to speak at the Covenant Service shortly after Ben's funeral. Was this the beginning of a call to preach? Chris and I talked it over, and we felt it was right that I should offer to go ahead with local preacher training, knowing full well that we were the assessors in this situation and that the Local Preachers' Meeting would not raise any objections – Chris was superintendent of the circuit by then, and it would have been very difficult to stop me! There is a lesson to be noted there about the power of the superintendent in Methodism, but we thought we were aware of the danger and were careful to take as many soundings as we could.

Simply being involved in church activities has never been enough for me, so my activities connected with the National Childbirth Trust gave me an outlet for the secular kind of ministry I felt called to. This was about rejoicing in new life, and supporting other people in the challenges it can bring. It was really good for me to have my own sphere of activity that was completely separate from the church, yet I felt that I was doing God's work in what I was offering other parents. It is rare to have a job where you know that what you are doing really is making an important difference to the people you are working with; I may not have been paid for it in material terms, but the rewards in job satisfaction were enormous.

From the outset, I had to be clear that Ben's life had not been in vain; to make sense of what had happened, and to survive personally, I had to look for some kind of good emerging from what appeared to be total desolation, while accepting also that there was much that would remain unfathomable. 'We know that all things work together for good for those who love God' (Romans 8.28) became my text for all time, alongside 'We love because he first loved us' (1 John 4.19), but the good had to be worked for and paid for in tears and heartbreak before it could be identified. As with the process of getting to know and understand myself, I slowly came to appreciate that there could be no short-cuts here either, and in fact would discover that in one important respect I had not even struggled – I had not, for a moment, doubted the existence of God, and only fleetingly questioned his love and trustworthiness. These really harrowing doubts came later.

8

Two Davids

It feels as if I have only begun to appreciate fully what it means to be human, and mortal, as a result of living through bereavements following the deaths of people I have loved. My father died when he was 76, after three months of real misery, because a major stroke had left him severely disabled with little quality of life. The overwhelming emotion at the time was one of relief that his suffering was over, and there was a sense that his dying was somehow in the scheme of things; he had managed to live beyond his allotted 'three score years and ten': 'The days of our life are seventy years, or perhaps eighty, if we are strong' (Psalm 90.10).

Traumatic though it was to lose Ben in the way we did, I think it was the death of my older brother, David, at the age of 57 that really brought to a head a whole string of questions, a reassessment of my priorities in life, and what my faith is based on, in a way which had not happened before, although the seeds had no doubt been sown in my earlier experiences. Quite possibly this was because he was my sibling; I could not help but identify very closely with someone who had shared so much of my childhood and family memories, and with whom so much could be taken for granted. It could also have had something to do with the fact that this was the only bereavement I have had where it was possible to find time and space for myself afterwards. Then, four months later, my brother-in-law, also David, died suddenly, plunging us straight into crisis mode again.

My brother David had special needs – but, as the headmaster of our children's school has often observed, we *all* have special needs. Today, David probably would have been diagnosed as having a form of Asperger's Syndrome, but in the 1950s, when he saw various specialists, this was a condition that was not recognized. It was a huge hurdle for him to survive his schooldays, and get the qualifications he needed to train as a nurse, although he had the most phenomenal memory when it came to dates, places, people – and train timetables. He was highly intelligent, but hated to be put on the spot in any way, and to be asked for a quick response was seen as a real threat. Familiar routines and an unhurried pace of life provided the best kind of environment for him, which is why he did so well when nursing older patients in the days when the National Health Service was not dealing with budget cuts and staff shortages to the extent that it does today.

Relationships within the family were often somewhat strained; my sister and I are accustomed to living life in the fast lane and are academically very able. David remained single, and was perceived by many as quite a solitary figure, although he loved to be in company when he felt safe and affirmed. Life was not easy for him, and it was something of a relief to us all when he was able to retire early on grounds of ill health. The pressure was off; he could spend his time as he wanted, which meant that he helped a lot with voluntary work at his church, and could devote himself to music and his model trains. He could be relied upon to write to his MP or local councillor if there were any issues about which he felt strongly, and he was a faithful correspondent on behalf of Amnesty International. A year before he died, he asked my family to come and hear him play Widor's *Toccata* on the organ at his church; he had been practising it for months, and it was a real triumph to hear him play it. In the world's eyes, he was not a great success story, but his last illness and death made me re-evaluate the person he was, what he stood for, and our relationship.

David had been diagnosed with non-Hodgkin's lymphoma ten years previously, and had lived pretty well with it. His first round of chemotherapy had nearly blown him away, and it was decided not to repeat such an aggressive course. He managed his subsequent treatments very well, and it was only two years before he died that he encountered real problems when he contracted shingles, which caused him acute pain in his face – his mouth and eyes were particularly badly affected. Nothing seemed to help the pain, and eventually we all agreed that he should no longer live on his own; we cleared his flat and he moved in to live with my mother, which was an arrangement that worked well – they could support each other in different ways, as my mother had fallen and broken her pelvis and was quite disabled. Then, in May 2002, the illness took a hold; he became very ill, struggling to breathe, and was admitted straightaway to hospital. My sister and I dropped everything and raced up to Edinburgh, where we met with the consultant who told us that this was now the start of the final stage of the illness; he suspected that David would live until the autumn, but nothing was certain. The initial thought was to help him with his breathing and then send him home, with the support of Macmillan nurses, because it was clear that my mother would not be able to cope on her own. We talked all this through with David; it was immensely helpful that we all knew the score, and could be open about his approaching death.

Ruth and I conferred, and worked out that we would travel up to Edinburgh on alternate weeks; curiously enough, it was easier for me, because I could fly from Stansted or Norwich, whereas the journey from Sheffield has to be done by road or train. Within a matter of days, David suffered a couple of strokes, which left him quite disabled, and there was no longer any thought of bringing him home. We began to ask about getting him a place in the hospice in Edinburgh, the Marie Curie Home, where our father had been the first chaplain some 30 years before. This was only a couple of miles away from our family home, and would make life much easier for my mother, who was finding the daily journey across Edinburgh to the hospital too much to sustain. We were incredibly fortunate in that a bed became vacant and David was moved quite quickly. The last ten days of his life were as happy and comfortable as we could have wanted – not least because the pain from the shingles in his face was dealt with at once.

When people came to visit him in the hospital, and then the hospice, it was very obvious how much he meant to them; this was their opportunity to give something in return for all the visits he had paid, and errands he had run for them. There was a sense of great peace and acceptance by his bedside; conversation was not really possible, but neither was it necessary. I was very struck by the way in which one visitor cared for him; although he did not, in fact, know David that well and was quite a recent friend, he seemed to know intuitively what was required and just sat, massaging David's feet for half an hour or so at a time.

I was fortunate in being on the spot on the day that David was transferred from the hospital to the hospice; it was a miserable, wet day, the ambulance had been delayed, and he was weary from waiting. It was very important to me that I was able to accompany him for the journey across Edinburgh, and this helped me to deal with the feelings of guilt for all the heedless and hurtful things I had said to him over the years; it felt like an occasion of reconciliation and resolution. I hope he understood. Thankfully Ruth was in Edinburgh when he actually died, and had been able to sit with him until late on the evening before. It was these spontaneous actions of human love and care which ultimately seemed to matter.

We had a private family service at the crematorium after David died, which we felt would be easier for us all, especially the children, then went on to his church for a Service of Thanksgiving. None of us had expected many people would come, but his minister had warned us that we might be surprised, as indeed we were when we arrived to find the church full. Well over a hundred people had come to show their love and respect for someone who had touched their lives in a variety of ways. There was no talk of pity or anything remotely patronizing here; something very powerful had been at work! As we left the church, the organist played Widor's *Toccata*, a fitting tribute to a person who had conquered enormous obstacles, and had won through in the end. We had included on the back of the order of service the passage from *Pilgrim's Progress* which tells of the summons of Mr Standfast, which expressed exactly how we felt about the way David had lived his life:

> Then there came forth a summons for Mr Standfast ... the contents whereof were, that he must prepare for a change of life, for his Master was not willing that he should be so far from Him any longer ... When Mr Standfast had thus set things in order, and the time being come to haste him away, he also went down to the river ...; wherefore Mr Standfast, when he was about half way in, stood a while, and talked to

his companions that had waited upon him thither. And he said, This river has been a terror to many; yea, the thoughts of it also have often frightened me; but now methinks I stand easy ... I see myself now at the end of my journey; my toilsome days are ended. I am going now to see that head that was crowned with thorns, and that face which was spit upon for me. I have formerly lived by hearsay and faith: but now I go where I shall live by sight, and shall be with Him in whose company I delight myself. I have loved to hear my Lord spoken of; and wherever I have seen the print of his shoe in the earth, there I have coveted to set my foot too.

(John Bunyan, *The Pilgrim's Progress*, pp. 305–6)

I returned home to my family, exhausted after the six weeks of weekly commuting between Edinburgh and Norfolk, during which time I had continued to work as usual. I hadn't dared to ask for time off, although it had been offered; we had no idea how long the last stage of the illness would last, and in fact the end came much more quickly than anyone had anticipated. When one is caught in that kind of situation, it is hard to ask for compassionate leave in case it is too early, and goodwill could be abused. But when it came to additional, voluntary activities, I had to make decisions on an *ad hoc* basis. I had been asked several months before to preach at a special service in Cambridge which involved the recognition of several new local preachers, one of whom was a good friend. The day before the service I rang up and cancelled, because I simply could not get my head around what I was supposed to be doing. In the event, David died the next day, and I was in Edinburgh. Shortly before this, I had attended an examiners' meeting in Cambridge; I drove straight down to Stansted afterwards, to catch the plane to Edinburgh. This would be the last time I saw David. With hindsight, I realize that this was pushing conscientiousness to its absolute limit: I was there for protocol only, another assessor for my paper was there, and I was really not needed. By the time I was back in Norfolk, it was late June, when the academic world calms down for a couple of months, so it was much easier to take up the offer of leave – and indeed I was so tired, I would not have been much use to anyone. This was very different from the period after Ben had died; I could stop, and I did, at least for two or three weeks – I guess I am too much of an activist to keep it up indefinitely!

As before, I was in a fog – but it was a strangely comforting kind of experience, as I felt enfolded in it, and in the love of my family, friends and colleagues. The peace from David's bedside was still tangible. The house was very quiet; Chris was away at the annual Methodist Conference for a week, and the children were at school. I knew that I had big questions, and was intrigued to observe that I could not face going to the beach, which is only three miles from our home. Previously, the sea had always been a real place of solace for me but during the weeks immediately after David's death, I was frankly scared to go – the space was too great, and my questions too enormous and threatening. It was safer to stay at home in our enclosed garden. This time I was not questioning the whereabouts of God, as I had before; I was much more concerned to sort out whether there was a God at all. Was the imagery of *Pilgrim's Progress* just a well-meaning myth?

> As she dies
> I struggle with my belief
> that there can
> be anything 'after'.

What an arrogant idea
that we are anything
other than animals
dying in our turn
to make room
for the next generation?

Was the whole gospel not simply a brilliant blend of fact and fiction, devised to help us develop as altruistic, compassionate human beings? How could my brother, a faithful Christian, have had such a difficult life, and then discover at the very end how much he was valued? Why did he have to suffer so much pain in the last two years, only to have it sorted out within days of arriving in the hospice? And how could I have gone so far through life without appreciating what really matters?

Perhaps I had reached a stage of sufficient security and maturity in my own faith that I now could dare to ask these kinds of questions, though it did not feel like it at the time. It was reminiscent of the time when I was grieving differently from Chris – an abyss had opened at my feet, and I was teetering on the edge. Over the next few months it was as if I had been given a rope ladder and I was able to let myself over the precipice, and could explore the chasm – God, or no God? Jesus Christ, incarnate, crucified, dead, buried and risen – or just mortal, and now very dead? I took no preaching appointments until I felt I had a faith worth sharing, and for a while I seriously wondered if I would ever preach again.

It was right that I stopped preaching in the period when I was particularly vulnerable; no congregation needs to be drawn into a preacher's deepest heart-searchings unless it is in a context where full and frank discussion can follow. I could not go along with Peter Boehler's advice to John Wesley: 'Preach faith till you have it; and then *because* you have it you *will* preach faith'. Wesley was reporting a particular discussion about faith and how it works; I was rather more at sea at this point, and preaching really was not an option, because I honestly did not know what, if anything, I believed. Preaching carries with it the authority of God and the Church, and I could not speak for either! Even when I was wrestling with fundamental doubts, I knew that just the act of going to church would make me vulnerable and likely to cry; I so wanted to believe and find comfort in the certainty of the resurrection, but could not find a short cut to hope. I could remember the times in the past when I had found solace and hope in church, and longed to experience that again. Anonymity might have been helpful; I could have tried to worship in another place where I was not known, or even wandered into a church during the week, but I was anxious to avoid a conversation with someone who might have seen my distress and wanted to help! Such is the isolation that can accompany vulnerability.

> Why, when I come to close to You
> in worship, or in prayer,
> do I want to weep?
> The tide of tears is there,
> pressing upwards
> inside of me,
> and rattling at my eyelids,
> and tickling my eyes.
>
> It's You I want to think about,
> to bring to You my love,
> and yet, inevitable and sure,
> the tears start to come
> and I am back,
> in the weeping place,
> and inside of me, trying once again
> to stem the tide.

Mostly it's the desolation and the loss
which consumes me,
but sometimes it seems
that this just reflects
the primeval desolation
that was there
even before
death took my love away.

Nothing that I read convinced me to believe again. Nor was it anything that was said to me, in conversation, or in church (when I went!). Gradually my belief returned, helped by the knowledge that many, many Christians have struggled over the generations with similar questions. I began to feel that my faith couldn't be alive and vibrant if I did not go back to root principles and question the absolute basics from time to time. But in the end it is a gift from God, not to be arrived at by a rational process of inquiry. I chose to take a step of faith, back into faith, but having looked carefully at what life would be like without it. The memory of my discovery of what really mattered as I sat at David's bedside, and the recognition of his faithful walk with God through a very difficult life, were key influences. Eventually, I decided that life without the God of love at the centre would not be worth living – Christ is what brings sense and hope to the world I know, and the world I anticipate, even though many questions are left unanswered.

Having taken the step back into faith, it was very liberating to have found that I could have doubts, and still believe. I do not have to provide myself, or anyone else, with clear answers to every question that might arise; I do not have to be certain. But I also have to be clear about where and when I air my uncertainties. It is a kind of boundaries question; there are places and times when it is perfectly in order, and other occasions when it isn't. Congregations may well prefer their ministers and preachers to be sure all the time, although it is not doing anyone any favours if they allow themselves to be regarded in this way. After Sarah's Service of Thanksgiving, some friends commented, 'We can just about understand why you decided not to have her baptized – after all, you know she will be a committed Christian when she grows up!' We were at pains to try to put them right and to point out that the chances were she might well reject it all, simply because of being a minister's child. They remained unconvinced. We are back to the pedestal image; it may be tempting to regard church leaders as being the fount of all knowledge and wisdom when it comes to matters of faith and Christian living, but what does that say about the leaders as human beings – and how does this help other people to grow in their faith? We all need to be given permission to ask the doubting questions.

Having more or less got my balance again, we returned to Edinburgh for a few days during the October half-term; as we were sitting on the top of a bus, Chris's mobile phone rang. It was Paul, his brother, ringing from Norwich, to say that he had just found their younger brother, David, dead in his flat. He had apparently suffered a massive heart attack. He was just 42. Our immediate reaction was one of disbelief – except we knew that Paul would never joke about something so serious. But this in itself was quite helpful, as it prepared us for the reactions of some people, especially in the circle of our children's schoolfriends – to lose one uncle is unfortunate, but to lose two in such quick succession is rather careless. When we had recovered our breath, we could reflect on the irony that I had been in Norwich when my brother died in Edinburgh, and we were in Edinburgh when Chris's brother died in Norwich. At the same time, we were grateful to the Methodist Church for listening to us when we had been due to move to a new circuit; we knew that both Davids had serious health problems, and recognizing the ages of our mothers, we had asked to be placed near one or other of our families and not either half-way between them or at the far end of the country. Had we been in York or Exeter, for example, life would have been extremely awkward.

Chris had been very fond of his brother, as we all had, although we did not live in each other's pockets. He was single, and lived in a council flat, so we had to move quickly to clear it. The joys of local council bureaucracy: we were told we had to have the flat clear by the Friday (David had died on Monday, and been found on Tuesday). We managed to gain a few more days' grace, but were out by the next Tuesday – then no one went near the flat for months! We had not known much about his life, although it became apparent as we worked in the flat that he had a lot of hobbies and interests. When it came to the funeral, we were pleasantly surprised to discover how many friends he had had, who took the trouble to come – friends from work, from his biking days, from his membership of the Royal Antediluvian Order of Buffaloes, and a variety of other contexts. David had not worked in recent years because of his heart condition and diabetes, but he had clearly made time for people, and had been ready to offer help when he could, rather like my brother. It meant a lot to us to discover this, because his life had not seemed particularly happy to us up to that point. Chris took the funeral service, which was a very positive experience, because of the real affection which people had clearly felt for David and which they shared with us before we went into the chapel (the undertaker was late, so there had been plenty of time to talk!). It certainly made a big difference to my mother-in-law;

she found she could lift her head up high, and take pride in the memory of the son who had caused her so much worry in the past.

Once again, our friends and colleagues were very supportive. Knowing that we were *expected* to take time to adjust to our new situation, and assimilate what had happened, was immensely reassuring. I should have been teaching, but a colleague rang up to insist that I should not even consider going to Cambridge; he would cover for me. It made it possible for us to take a few days off and help sort out David's effects, and finances. The family needed to talk; my mother-in-law felt very helpless because she was more or less housebound, and she was in shock; our children were stunned, and somewhat disorientated by it all. Two uncles dying in four months was a hard introduction to bereavement, and it was important to take time to listen and to talk. Simply having the pressure of 'business as normal' lifted off our shoulders made it possible to start dealing with the various issues we had to face, rather than putting it off until the next holiday.

Of course, there are aspects to both Chris's work and mine that we can do more or less on autopilot, such as routine administration which does not require emotional energy or creative thought; unfortunately, however, this is the kind of work that is most easily farmed out when offers of help come rolling in! It is the public things that are more difficult. There are no hard and fast rules about this; everyone has to respond in the way that is right for them, at that particular time. The important thing is to make that decision because of one's own wishes and sense of what is right, and not to feel manipulated to meet the expectations of others. The old adage that no one is indispensable is helpful, even if it can be an uncomfortable lesson for those of us who like to think that the world will stop if we are not there to manage it.

I don't think I am unusual in my preference for leading an ordered life, which I control. My children would probably argue that I am too organized for their liking, but that is another story! When facing bereavement, order disappears; for me it was like being adrift with no charts, and no outboard motor, but simply at the mercy of the wind and the waves. It didn't take long to recognize that when I eventually reached land again, it would be a different place from the part I had left, and that there could be no going back. The idea of things 'returning to normal' was simply pie in the sky, with no relation to reality; I would have to find a new normality, a new way of living with the presence of the loss – which is not a complete contradiction in terms. Fortunately, I was not left to do this on my own.

9

Moving On

I sense a basket of light
Woven around me
In this darkness deeper than night
Keeping me from descending
Into the pit.

They say that man is made
In the image of God
And that the light that does not fade
Is the Spirit
Indwelling.

A soft and gentle glowing
Is the light from each heart
That keeps me from growing
Self-centred and
Apart.

Long ago, a woman made
A basket of rushes
And in it gently laid her son
To float upon
The Nile

And so, like a basket of light
Woven around me
In this darkness deeper than night
Is the God-side of people
And I give thanks.

Without the 'God-side' of people, moving on
would have been impossible for me. The way in which
family and friends, and others who were not so close,

related to me during the dark days, weeks and months of bereavement were of the utmost significance. Some seemed to know instinctively what would be helpful, others no doubt agonized about what to say or do; some got it right in my eyes, and some got it hideously wrong. What found an echo in my heart would not necessarily work for the next person, even if the situation seemed similar. We are all individual!

Some things, however, stand out as being particularly important. At the very beginning, only an hour or so after Ben's death, we needed other people to be able to acknowledge what had happened. When I was moved from the delivery room into a side ward, we passed a nurse in the corridor. She turned away, unable to catch our eyes; it was obvious that she knew, and did not know how to respond, so she avoided us. In the delivery room we had been in a strangely safe environment, almost womb-like in its own right. This was where our son had briefly been part of our world, although he had never opened his eyes; this was where the nurses and doctors had willed him to live, and where we had held him, where Chris had baptized him, and where he died. No explanations were necessary while we were cocooned in that small space, but of course we had to move on elsewhere to free up the room – and face the world, which felt alien, and threatening. Our first encounter outside was not encouraging.

As far as I can remember, that experience was not repeated. People may have felt awkward in our presence, but never tried to avoid us; that was surprising in a way, and a real accolade for the community in Wensleydale. There were occasions when I was the one to take evasive action, because I simply could not face seeing someone or speaking to them, and I fear that I may well have caused offence.

I can only hope that they understood I was in a very fragile place. It should have been a lesson to me about how easy it is to judge people unfairly – but it is a lesson I am still learning!

Finding the right words to say must have been a challenge; I know how I hesitate now to say anything to someone in crisis because of my fear of making things worse. Looks, and touch, meant a great deal; one day, someone crossed the street from the other side of the market place in Hawes, and grasped my arm. They did not say a word, but the action said it all. Friends came to see us, and sat in silence; one or two cried, and their tears were a comfort. It meant that they were identifying with our grief, and standing next to us in our pain. One friend came through atrocious weather conditions with her family from Leeds; she sent her husband and children off to explore the town, and then sat with her arms around me. The only conversation I can remember was her offer to make a cup of tea! The book of Job is famous partly because of the ineptitude of Job's comforters, who caused him more hurt when they tried to explain to him why his afflictions had happened. But at the very beginning we are told they said nothing: 'They sat with him on the ground for seven days and seven nights, and no one spoke to him, for they saw his suffering was very great' (Job 2.13). Waiting for him to speak first was actually a very helpful and sensitive thing to do, even if they were only conforming to the traditions of their society.

But ours is a verbal culture, and many people cannot cope with silence. Gaps in the conversation are spaces that have to be filled, and this is where clichés come into their own. Although they often express quite profound truths, the sheer fact that they are expressed so often can make them sound hollow. Situations surrounding bereavement seem to be fertile ground for them. I did not appreciate being told, as I was on several occasions, 'I know exactly how you feel.' How could they? And how dare they assume that they knew? How could they possibly understand where I was at that particular point of that particular day, on the roller coaster of emotions which was grief?

'Time heals – you will feel much better after a year or so.' Well, maybe; but somehow I had to get through *today*. And I didn't particularly want time to heal, because the pain was a link with the person I was mourning. Not to feel pain would be disloyal to them. Unlike being ill, when one longs to feel better, learning to live with grief is more complicated. Anniversaries (and there are many) matter enormously. One friend remembered the date when Ben was actually due, and made sure she saw me that day.

'Christians should never be depressed.' How often have I heard this said, in a range of situations? It makes me angry, because it is a particularly dangerous thing to say, denying the suffering that grief involves, and which is a necessary part of the process of finding a new way forward. It may also stop someone going for help when they need it, because they feel guilty and inadequate. No one ever said it to my face, but I sensed impatience in some, because I was not 'getting over' Ben as quickly as they thought I should, and I felt the pressure of expectations that my faith should surely help me deal with it. Is there not an important place in the Bible and in Christian tradition, for songs of lament? And it is not just human beings who experience desolation; for me a God who cannot suffer is indeed insufferable (Davies, *The Vigilant God*, p. 115).

Some things that people said were dismissive and hurtful, often involving comparisons that were thoroughly unhelpful. The registrar saying to Chris, when he went in with Sarah to register Ben's death, 'Never mind, you can always have another, and at least you have one already,' seemed to deny his existence and place in our lives. After their uncles' deaths, the children at school were faced with, 'It's not like you lost your Mum or your Dad, is it?' In complete contrast, another child said to Sarah: 'I'm here if you want to talk – it must be really hard for you,' a rare gesture of concern and empathy from a teenage peer which meant a great deal. The children's experience in general demonstrated how inadequate people may feel in the face of someone else's grief, and embarrassment can lead to some very inept comments.

Then there were the overtly religious statements, such as, 'But you know your loved one is in heaven, and better off than they could ever be here with you.' We said this ourselves in the letter we sent out that Christmas – it was one thing to say it, but quite another to have it said to us! Here we were, face to face with our own efforts to make sense of what was happening and I, for one, did not respond very well. It almost felt as if my bluff was being called, and I did not perform as I should have done, or was expected to do. The text from Romans 8.38–39 was sometimes cited, which *did* mean a lot to me – but I had to get there myself, at my own pace, and own it. It simply was no good to be told these truths by someone else, in perhaps a slightly too glib manner. My arms were aching with emptiness for Ben, I kept seeing David in the living room, garden, or street, and I missed them, and wanted them there, with me, then.

Spoken words may not always have been particularly helpful. But words spoken in prayer, perhaps even unarticulated thoughts, were something completely different. When I could not even think of praying, other than occasionally through the words of the Psalms, it was a great comfort to know that others were continuing, on our behalf. 'The prayer of the righteous is powerful and effective' (James 3.16), and we experienced this again and again. It was as if our friends and family were able to keep us in a safe place, supported by the love of God, where hurt and rawness were recognized and healing could slowly begin. Prayer could be identified in actions as well; the gift of mince pies on the day Ben died, the meal-on-wheels which appeared on New Year's Eve, the willingness of friends to look after Sarah, or do the ironing, the availability of bereavement counselling, the holiday in Majorca, the care shown to David – all revealed God's hands at work on earth, channelling his love and care in our direction.

This could almost be seen as a cosy place to wallow, reminiscent of the hippopotamus in Flanders and Swan's famous song. There came a time when we had to move on, out of the safe place, and into the mainstream of life. For us this came in stages; the first was almost immediate, with the funeral marking the end of the phase of public mourning, when we had been expected and allowed to retreat from normal life and concentrate on ourselves and what needed to be done. Kingsley Barrett's sermon put down some markers for us as to how we might proceed; he talked of the importance of reason, steadiness and courage, which we would need if our lives were going to have a positive direction in the future. He also put Ben's death into a theological perspective that gave us hope and encouragement. He spoke out of his own faith, conviction and integrity; this was not just pie in the sky and wishful thinking, to try to make us feel better. Coming from one of my father's closest friends, and someone whom I had come to love and respect during my student days, this meant a great deal.

I would not like to hazard even a guess as to when the move was complete; this would be almost to imply that there came a point when grief was 'over', and the process finished. I am sure this did not happen; it certainly is not something I would recognize. However, there were some clear milestones along the way to reaching a point of acknowledging that we were becoming used to a new normality; we were in the swim of things again, although not 'back' in the swim. Our return from Majorca was one of these points; for the first time we could think about the future with some degree of energy and hope. Life had begun to show some piquancy again, instead of giving the impression of being like a bowl of particularly sticky porridge.

We could not have reached that point without the help of our friends, who saw the need to intervene and make something happen. Two particular sets of people were prepared to take courage in both hands, and risk our rejection, or even anger, when they became involved. It is so much easier and safer to settle for offering tea and sympathy than it is to suggest that the time may have come to confront the situation, and do something to change it! The first was our doctor, who kept close tabs on us; he saw us very regularly because of Sarah's health problems, which could almost be seen as a blessing in disguise, although I have to admit that it is only as I write this that I have come to see them in that light. He could see the depth of my depression, and how tired and pressurized Chris was, and told us that we should think very seriously about accepting the offer of bereavement counselling. His advice was acceptable because he was someone we both respected and trusted. He was also prepared to take on the wrath of the consultant in the ear, nose and throat department at the hospital, when he disagreed with his advice not to fly. I guess that must have taken some courage.

Ken and June Hebborn were the other catalyst. We were in regular communication and I am sure they would not have dared to intervene in the way they did, with the cheque from their prayer group and the instruction to 'Go away and get well!' if they had not felt they had a good idea as to what was actually happening in our lives. This was a risky thing to do, as it might have been seen as bringing yet another pressure to bear on us, and particularly on Chris, just at a point when additional stress was not needed. It might also have been seen as an attempt to intervene in our lives. But we were at such a low point that someone did indeed need to step in and take the initiative. As it was, they had known Chris for many years, they gauged it exactly right, and we were able to recognize their gift as an answer to prayer. Their action, coming as we decided to follow the doctor's advice and approach Hilary, made it possible to take the plunge.

The support of friends and family while I have learned to live with loss has helped me to understand much more about what it means to be human. Doubts about mortality, immortality, vulnerability and trust have all had to be addressed – and they constantly reappear, to be thought about again. The boxes have not simply been ticked! Closely linked to these are questions concerning the Christian journey, the ministry to which we are all called as disciples, and public ministry; the public nature of being both a local preacher and married to an ordained person has had an impact on me, whether I like it or not. I am on my own particular pilgrimage, which has come about because I am the unique individual that I am; no one else will have the same experience, regardless of how apparently similar their circumstances may be. I have written about people and situations that have helped and hindered me as I have adjusted to living with loss; but this is not meant to be a blueprint for how it should be. Everyone will have a unique story to tell.

There are various support organizations which may be helpful, and the names and addresses are listed at the end of the book. Many of them publish newsletters; personally I found these to be both interesting and helpful, in that we were able to understand more about Ben's condition and the incidence of Trisomy cases in Britain. We continued to get the Support Organisation For Trisomy 13/18 newsletter for several years after his death. I greeted its arrival with mixed feelings, knowing that it would make harrowing reading, yet it was good to share other people's stories, and to be able to empathize with them. I would pick a time when I knew the house would be empty for a few hours, sit down with a cup of coffee and a good supply of tissues, and read; it was quite a cathartic process.

Many organizations offer helpline support, which is useful, particularly if there is no other help immediately available. Sometimes it is good to be able to talk to someone whom you have never met, and are not likely to meet in the future. Anonymity can be liberating! I found it helpful to keep leaflets about the Stillbirth and Neonatal Death Society with me for many years, because I got so many enquiries about late miscarriages and neonatal deaths; it seemed more caring to be able to put a leaflet straight into someone's hands, than to give them the address or phone number. Perhaps that says something about me, and the desire to do some problem-solving. It is so hard to watch another person struggle, and the temptation is strong to try to make things better for them.

In the end, however, there are no quick-fix solutions. Each one of us has to make their own journey through bereavement, either as someone who is in the process of learning to live with loss, or as someone who cares for a person who has been bereaved, because it is a journey for them too. If this book has provided companionship on that journey, then it has done its job.

Contemporary Practice

An Afterword by Gail Kerry, Assistant Hospital Chaplain, The Queen Elizabeth Hospital, King's Lynn, Norfolk

As a hospital chaplain I seldom have the opportunity to hear the ongoing story of the parents whose lives I suddenly become involved in. Esther's story has for me been both informative regarding what may happen in the years that follow a bereavement, but also very moving as she has endeavoured to share her pain and the impact Ben has made on her life.

Chris and Esther were mature adults when Ben died and had both had a lot of experience in ministry, but they, like many others who find themselves in a similar situation, had no previous experience to draw on as to how to deal with Ben's death. Not surprisingly they looked back on their grieving and wondered if they could have done things differently. But society as a whole has moved on regarding the subject of stillbirth and pre-viable deaths. Fifty years ago the event happened but few people spoke of it. Nowadays much has changed. The debates about abortion, infertility treatment, the ethics of genetic research, etc. have enabled society to talk about the early stages of life and when life begins. There is also an increasing openness about expressing our feelings. But all of us need others alongside us to facilitate this.

Nowadays, as a consequence of having scans, the majority of abnormalities are found before delivery and hence a lot of discussion will already have taken place with medical staff. Every hospital will have various ways of helping parents – help given through medical staff, through counsellors and from the chaplaincy department. What follows is not a list of what can or should be done on each occasion, but all are a means of helping people to acknowledge and express their grief. It is important to treat parents as individuals and respond to their need.

Staff in the hospital aim to involve a chaplain as soon as possible after the mother has come into hospital whether the circumstance is a termination for foetal abnormality, a stillbirth, or a miscarriage. This is for two practical reasons – it is not fair to be talking to someone when she is in labour, particularly if she is in pain; and to have a stranger come in and talk once the baby has been born does not sit comfortably with us. As chaplains we are very much aware that a lot is going on and many decisions have to be made. Esther expressed how in the hospital it was hard to know what to do; it was the same when she and Chris began thinking about a funeral. We try to give as much time and space as possible to a parent or parents so that they can think through their needs. We are there for the parents but also to be alongside medical staff for whom the event is so very opposite to all they have been trained to do.

Esther and Chris were very fortunate in that they were moved to a side ward after Ben was born. This did not always happen. Many hospitals nowadays have a special room or rooms so that the mother is not in the main delivery area. These rooms are equipped with such things as a sofa bed, en suite shower, facilities for making tea and coffee, etc. The room will be available to them as long as they need it. These facilities allow a family to have time and space to take in what is happening.

As I read Esther's story two things stood out as being important factors for her at the time of Ben's birth and death an hour later. First, Esther had to find the courage to see Ben. There is an appreciation of this and so staff find ways of helping parents. They can describe what the baby looks like, for our imaginations can be very inventive. The baby will be wrapped in a blanket and so the parents can gradually unwrap the blanket at their own pace. Or the baby can be placed in a Moses basket by the bed until the parents are ready to look. Parents will always be given plenty of time and it is not unusual for the baby to be with the parent/parents until the next day.

Then there is the fact expressed by Esther that no one other than Chris and herself, and the medical staff, saw Ben. We recognize that not everyone will feel able to come and see the baby, but others will want to. Family and friends may be able to visit. In Esther and Chris's situation we would have asked them if they would have liked someone to bring Sarah in. Although very young, and not able to understand what was happening, there could have been a sense for all of them that she had seen her brother and shared the experience. We do warn parents, however, that young children can ask very direct and blunt questions because they have no concept of the reality of death. Although parents find it very hard to explain to young children what has happened, it is better if it is in their own words; but we do have books available that parents can read to young children.

This sharing of the experience seems to be vitally important not just for the parents but also for the wider family. Although their shared experiences of Ben would have been brief – i.e. the time in hospital and the funeral – it would nevertheless have enabled them to grieve together. Personal time together as a family, without the need to 'put on a face for the funeral', is a precious time.

Although Chris and Esther had very little time with Ben they did have a photograph of him; today parents are encouraged to take their own photographs. If the decision is made not to see the baby, the photographs will be kept in the medical records so that they can be seen at a later date, if they so wish. Nowadays hand and footprints are also taken and name tags given to the parents. Because when a baby dies there are very few memories, everything that is done seems to have added importance. One way of grieving is to have a memory box, which can be used to help children grieve. In the box can be placed such things as the hand and footprints and the photographs. If the baby has enough hair a lock can be taken and put in the box.

As the date for Ben's birth drew closer, Esther recalls washing the first-size baby clothes. They found it helpful to ask the undertaker to dress him in something he had been given; in this hospital we have a whole wardrobe of clothes for very tiny babies which parents are able to choose from. They could have gone to the undertaker's and dressed him themselves, if they had so wished. In the case of a burial, toys and other objects may also be placed in the coffin.

Parents often have a real need to express and do something special for their baby and this sometimes takes the form of a simple religious gesture, perhaps by having a naming and blessing service. Esther expressed this sentiment. Chris baptized Ben as much for their sake as for his, for as Christians they knew it wasn't his passport to heaven. Esther and Chris needed to show that they loved him. He was special to them and also special to God. Our practice as chaplains can vary from simple extempore prayers to using words from a service book, or parents can choose something to be read. Parents might want the event to be just with themselves and the chaplain; often medical staff are present and sometimes the wider family gathers together. We may ask the parents to think about whether they want other children to be present, even those who are quite small. The unit has a baptismal bowl and stand. Baptismal or blessing cards, together with candles, are also given. Because there are very few concrete reminders of the child, it becomes important to have these signs of their life. Rituals and rites of passage come into their own at times of strong emotion as they help to unite all those gathered and bring comfort beyond words. They help to put the event into context with other important life events.

Time is also a precious commodity. Parents are given time to be with their baby, not just on their own but so that family can visit if they so wish. Deciding when to leave their baby and how to do it is very important and this is discussed. Chris and Esther left the hospital utterly empty. In some cases it is possible for parents to take their baby home for a short while. Esther says she was not sure she could or would have wanted to. A lot of discussion takes place before this happens and parents also have to sign a form saying they will return the baby to the hospital.

There is no legal requirement to have a funeral before 24 weeks but increasingly there is a desire to have one. As with hospital practice, the local situation regarding funerals will vary from area to area. A funeral can be either a burial or a cremation. Families can arrange the funeral privately, as with any other death, or the hospital chaplain can be involved. Chris and Esther's decision to have a funeral for Ben in the same manner as for anyone else may have been unusual then, but not so now. Many churches now have in their liturgy a service for a stillborn child. But as with any funeral service, the family concerned has a say in what they would like to happen. For a baby who has died at birth, the funeral is one of the few things the parent can do, for so much else has been denied them. Possibly because Chris was a Methodist minister and accustomed to taking funeral services, and Esther a Christian, they were able to think about what they wanted for Ben's funeral service and why.

Many people, of course, would not be in this position and would need support and to be given ideas as to what is possible or desirable. The undertaker, who was also a friend, carried Ben's coffin, which made it feel very natural, and this may be very important for someone in the family to do. Flowers can be brought to the service. Instead of scattering soil on the coffin at a burial, it may be that a flower is taken from a wreath; alternatively a basket can be brought to the service with rose petals or dried flowers, and these are scattered by those attending the service. A candle may also be given to mark the day. What is of the utmost importance is that real choices can be made. Esther recalled the moment of near hysteria when they entered the chapel to Brahms' *Lullaby*. But some families choose this.

For Esther and Chris the pain will always be real, for however much medical staff and chaplains, family and friends, offer support and care, the loss of Ben remains. Whatever practical things we do to help parents to grieve, what they will always need is people who are willing to stand beside them in their pain. The place of pain and grief is a dark and scary place, but as Psalm 139.12 says: 'Even the darkness is not dark to you.' God may have appeared hidden to Esther and Chris, but they were not hidden from God.

Useful Addresses

The Compassionate Friends
Support for bereaved parents and their families
53 North Street
Bristol BS3 1EN
Tel: 08451 203785
Helpline: 08451 232304
E-mail: info@tcf.org.uk
www.tcf.org.uk

CRUSE Bereavement Care
Cruse House
126 Sheen Road
Richmond
Surrey TW9 1UR
Tel: 020 8939 9530
Helpline: 0870 167 1677
E-mail: helpline@crusebereavementcare.org.uk
www.crusebereavementcare.org.uk

The Miscarriage Association
c/o Clayton Hospital
Northgate
Wakefield
West Yorkshire WF1 3JS
Tel: 01924 200795
Helpline: 01924 200799
Scottish helpline: 0131 334 8883
E-mail: info@miscarriageassociation.org.uk
www.miscarriageassociation.org.uk

S.O.F.T. (UK)
Support Organisation For Trisomy 13/18 and related
disorders
Tel: 0121 351 3122
E-mail: enquiries@soft.org.uk
www.soft.org.uk

**Stillbirth and Neonatal Death Society
(SANDS)**
28 Portland Place
London W1B 1LY
Helpline: 020 7436 5881
E-mail: support@uk-sands.org
www.uk-sands.org

References and Select Bibliography

John Bunyan, *The Pilgrim's Progress*, London, Lutterworth Press, 1947.

Horton Davies, *The Vigilant God: Providence in the Thought of Augustine, Aquinas, Calvin and Barth*, New York, Peter Lang Publishing, 1992.

Derek Kidner, *Psalms 73–150*, London, Inter-Varsity Press, 1975.

Alister McGrath (ed.), *Modern Christian Thought*, Oxford, Blackwell, 1993.

Methodist Church, *Hymns & Psalms*, London, Methodist Publishing House, 1983.

Methodist Worship Book, Peterborough, Methodist Publishing House, 1999.

Pam Vredevelt, *Empty Arms*, Oregon, Multnomah Press, 1984.

Gordon Wakefield, *Methodist Spirituality*, Peterborough, Epworth Press, 1999.

Agnes Whitaker (ed.), *All in the End is Harvest*, London, Darton, Longman and Todd, 1984.

Roy Zuck, *Job*, Chicago, Moody Press, 1978.